Terry Godwin

o o o

Come Fly with Me

PublishAmerica

Baltimore

First printing

ISBN: 1-4137-9746-6
PUBLISHED BY PUBLISHAMERICA, LLLP
www.publishamerica.com
Baltimore

Printed in the United States of America

Contents

The Dance of Life

Every thing begins at birth,
The day we arrive on earth.
Picking our parents, a very wise thing to do
Then begins the dance of life without further ado.

Absorbing the rhythm of your mother's love,
Snuggling close as a good fitting glove.
You grow, become aware that you have a dad,
A benefit of which most families will be glad.

A few years on, you learn to move around.
Placing your feet firmly on the ground
Then one day you realise the safeness of earth's floor,
On the world of which we hope you will come to adore.

Every day that passes you learn much more,
The stronger you grow the more you wish to explore.
You learn to depend on those who love you,
In turn you must respond to love them too.

Leaving childhood and becoming a young adult,
You scan the big outside world for every fault
Each day you wonder whether to stride ahead,
Or nervously dither, stand still, or be cautiously led.

Today, so many opportunities, all so inviting,
The dance of life for the young is so exciting.
Think positive and the world can be your oyster,
Think negative and be confined to your cloister.

The rhythm of life will urge you to mate,
Mother Nature will encourage you to keep that date.
Its seems our world itself must perpetuate,
And its population must regenerate.

With a family in tow the dance goes on,
It gives you a purpose to work upon.
It demands of your love, care and dedication,
And can bring you great sorrow or elation.

The family has matured and grown.
Your progeny in the nest now has flown.
Your partner and you can now enjoy a life of your own,
Your life in the future is set by the seeds you have sown.

Our new found freedom allows us to stand and stare,
Thinking of how to enjoy our future life and where.
The end of the dance may be near or far,
Whatever, don't let despondency your future happiness mar.

The dance of life probably now has a slower beat,
Less challenges you will have to meet.
It's vital to retain your "get up and go"
Keep Father Time at bay, that ever watchful so and so.

Rest and relax, enjoy the calm, the setting of the evening sun,
You have played your part in life, your span is nearly done.
If life was good, we hope it has been a happy one,
If was hard, then blessed relief you will be happy to come.

The silence has told the dance has stopped, it's run its race,
The dancer has retired with dignity and grace.
In death, your loved ones will honour you on bended knee,
Praying you go to heaven for eternity.

We know not the purpose of the "Dance of Life," unless it is to drive us on,
With ups and downs, its disasters, its glories, new birth, ever moving the world along.
Since this universe was created its vitality has been driven
To respond to the "Dance of Life," its beat and perpetual rhythm.

The Blue Teapot

A young newlywed Indian civil servant seeks accommodation
Not finding it he is on the point of desperation.
There is so little about to rent
He is exhausted, seeking a home, all energy spent.

His mother advised him to see the Holy man
To help him out of this situation if he can.
"I need a small apartment, three rooms will do,
With kitchen, bathroom and a balcony too."

The Holy man said, "Take this incense and burn
It in a little blue teapot and in turn
A genie will appear who will make your wish come true."
Quickly our newlywed did what he was told to do.

Sure enough a genie appeared and said, "What is your command
Let me know, and I will try to meet your demand."
"I need a small apartment, three rooms will do
With kitchen, bathroom and a balcony too."
The genie replied, "You may think you are not asking a lot
But if I could help you I wouldn't be living in this blue teapot!"

Hark

Hark, I hear the ice crack, the Spring melt has begun,
Ice and snow disappear under a gentle sun.
Hark, I hear the increase of a flowing stream,
The Spring's breezes are still a little keen.

Hark, I hear our feathered friend's glorious trill,
Responding to the awakening earth, life's thrill.
Hark, I hear the roll of thunder on the mount,
Bringing in showers on which nature does count.

Hark, I hear newborn lambs bleating with their flock,
Winter's passed, no turning back the clock.
Hark, I hear the ploughing of the field by tractor,
Ensuring our harvest—an essential factor.

Hark, I hear the frogs croaking beside pond and lawn,
Securing future generations with their spawn.
Hark, I hear the splashing fish leaping with acceleration,
Spring is in the air, they are full of anticipation.

Hark, I hear the enticing laughter of young girls,
Capturing their lovers with smiles and curls.
Hark, listen to the World, stand and stare,
Because Mother Nature is blossoming everywhere.

A Beautiful Woman

Mother Nature decrees that ladies have the right to be beautiful,
So that men should admire, desire, woo and be gentle and dutiful.
At the beginning Mother Nature decreed that men should be the stronger sex,
Since we have become more civilised that is going out of context.

The beauty of the woman is to enable her to entice her man,
To mate, have children is Nature's plan.
The man to be the provider and defender of the family,
To care and love with all his capability.

But now in this modern and growing world
Womanhood is safe, and many opportunities are now unfurled.
Where brains not brawn are the criteria,
Women compete with men and prove they are not their inferior.

In the woman's genes Nature wants her to mate,
To have children is her mandate.
Now she has time to seek her man and select,
To see if he is suitable in every aspect.
She has independence not available in the past,
With careful planning she can make it last.
Now the fortunes of women have improved for the better,
She still dreams of the day when she will send her letter,
Inviting you all to her white wedding and unification
To the man she loves and completing Mother Nature's expectation.

Forever

Old Father Tyme, when Mother Earth was born created "Forever"
To frustrate mankind, whether dull, sad, happy or clever.
Tomorrow never comes, of that you can be sure,
Perhaps it is that uncertainty that gives it that allure.

Back in the age of the "Very, very long ago"
Our great, great grandfathers realised it was so.
That the time it took to complete matters was "Forever"
Even they came to the end of their tether.

In this modern world everything is done with speed in mind
Anything slow, dull or awkward is a bane to mankind.
When plans go askew, disruptions occur, however
Old Father Tyme steps in, and we wait forever and ever.

In our effort to get there and back in the shortest time
The human race has developed road rage—a terrible crime.
The driver sits in a traffic jam in a vehicle built for speed,
His frustration ignores anyone else's need.

Civilisation advances each day, and so does our frustration
Old Father Tyme may have produced "Forever," its cause our creation.
Every day, where civilisation has taken its hold,
Innumerable stories of bureaucracy, delay, taking "Forever" are told.

Hospital lists are getting longer, government administration increases daily,
Traffic jams are more frequent, planning departments ignore reason gaily.
Timetables at airports and railway stations are askew,
At petrol pumps, super store tills, post offices, banks, you stand and queue.

Our list of frustrations could go on and on
Rather sad our society has to sing such a song.
Old Father Tyme has endowed us with "Forever"
But to combat that, God blessed us with patience and endeavour.

Come Fly with Me and See the World

I dreamed a dream that I could fly,
I dreamed I could fly high into the sky,
I dreamed of resting on a beautiful white cloud,
I dreamed it would be my throne with which I had been endowed.

That the winds had been placed under my command,
When on my cloud, now my chariot, to move me on demand.
I could travel with the sun and always enjoy the light of day,
I would avoid the thunder clouds, lightning, storms, and keep out of harm's way.

I have read books of travel, listened to the traveller's tales of glory,
Now I could see what they had seen and relate my own story.
I will glide over mountains glistening with snow,
Leaving no footprints on the land I pass over below.

I will thrill when I arrive over the African Plains,
Marvelling at the multitude of animals awaiting the seasonal rains.
The Amazon Basin with its torrential weather and evergreen forest,
Its fauna, its floribunda, its invertebrate attracting universal interest.

I want to fly to the poles North and South, both very cold,
Where the Arctic weather is a terror in itself to behold.
Where polar bears to survive sleep the winter through,
Where seals live under the ice floes, incredible but true.

I want to see the camel trains plodding over the Sahara's burning sand
To see the sunsets and dawns that are a breath taking sight, simply grand!
To follow the course of the River Nile, the longest river in the world.
On its banks, the Pyramids and its mysteries to be unfurled.

I want to see and feel the might and power of the Niagara Falls,
To study and appreciate the building of the famous "China Walls."
To coast along the great Himalayan Mountain Range,
Passing over Everest, the highest, the greatest will surely be strange!

To flow along and through the Grand Canyon, a wonder of renown,
Its grandeur, its depth and length entitles it to its own crown.
There are so many of the world's marvels I must go and see,
Dear Lord, please don't wake me up or this wonderment will never come to be.

Castles in the Air

I remember when my dad was down, disappointed and sad,
He would dream of his Castle in the Air, and that would make him glad.
I never knew how he came to own such an estate,
But when he visited it, his worries would soon dissipate.

A Castle in the Air is pure imagination,
Building one takes time and determination.
It takes a strong will to stand up and fight
Against failure, regret, criticism, and above all the darkness of the night.

A Castle in the Air is ones shelter in a welcoming haven,
When the world makes you feel unwanted and craven.
It's where you look for a smile and signs of hope
Making tomorrow another day in which you can cope.

Your Castle in the Air is your belief
That your inner strength can bring you welcome relief.
When the world appears against you, causing you grief,
Enjoy your life in full, don't let worry and misery be a time thief.

Build your Castle in the Air, value it all your life
Let it help you to reduce trouble and strife.
Make it your touchstone to enjoy the world you live in,
You will be a blessing to the world, your friends and all your kin.

Autumn

When Winter comes, can Spring be far behind
Is an ancient and true saying you will find.
In Winter the sun and warmth quickly disappear
On the windows continuous raindrops we hear.

The days become shorter and grey skies dominate
Winds and gales blow through at a steady rate.
Jack Frost sticks in his long icy finger
And dreary Winter seems to linger and linger.

Then comes what the World has been waiting for
Brisk bustling and sparkling Spring knocks on the door.
Thrusting buds push up from under the snow
Frisky new born lambs set our hearts aglow.

The farmers plough the field and sew the seed
To provide the food that the human race will need.
Flowers asleep through Winter's long chill night
Gush in profusion and colour—what a gorgeous sight.

Summer sidles in gentle breezes, blue skies, warmer days
We enjoy rambling walks along the country ways.
Nights are cut short as daylight takes over
And green becomes Nature's most prolific colour.

To be in England's green and pleasant land
In our Summer can be "Oh, oh so grand."
Never too hot or too cold, never too extreme
Summer glides away, so quickly does it seem.

Autumn is the season I love best of all
It is the occasion of our Harvest Festival.
The fruits of this good earth are all set out
To nourish the world, that's what it's all about.

The ground becomes covered in leaves gold and red
As the trees and shrubs prepare for their Winter bed.
The nights draw in, the earth cools down
Evening lamps light early in the busy town.

The logs are split for the home-side fire
Whose dancing and flickering flames I never tire.
When Autumn comes, Winter awaits in the hall
Nevertheless, I will always love Autumn best of all.

The Day the Earth Trembled

On December 26 the grim reaper visited Earth with zest,
On that day his killings were one of his highest.
His Tsunami slaughtered two hundred and fifty thousand at a stroke,
His deadly agent among the innocents ran amok.

The world trembled when his Tsunami was set free,
It roared across the oceans in a deadly spree.
No warning was given, to maximise its devastating effect,
It was to those innocents death direct.

Those left alive in the Tsunami's terrible wake
Smashed, injured, broken, those whom the gods did forsake.
Loved ones, homes, everything that human life needed,
The Tsunami obliterated it all, it completely succeeded.

The grim reaper has left a fearsome aftermath,
Ensuring the death total would keep on its upward graph.
With no water, food, sanitation or medication,
The surviving innocents couldn't be in a worse situation.

The stunned world is slowly reacting to this horrific disaster,
Support must be immediate, and aid must be given faster.
An epidemic on a gigantic scale will soon raise its heinous head.
More and more and more innocents will soon be dead.

This is a catastrophe the world has not seen the like of before,
We must all act generously to try and save and restore
The human race now standing at deaths door

*At the time this poem was written, the death toll stood at fifty thousand
and has been upgraded accordingly.*

Mum, Why Did You Marry Dad?

I sat by the quiet lakeside, it was evening, with my daughter,
We were admiring the sunset on the still calm water.
In a fortnight's time we would be hearing the sound of wedding bells,
We had been planning this event, trying not to break any shells.
After a few minutes of quiet contemplation
Mary asked a question that required consideration.
"Mum, why did you marry Dad?"
That enquiry before I never had.

George and I had been married over thirty year,
My memories of our marriage were treasured and dear.
Yes I was a woman who wanted to be a wife,
I wanted a husband and family to be the centre of my life.
Yes I wanted a home, security and love,
We all want happiness and companionship and above
All, health and strength and stability to get us through
Any hard times ahead enabling the family to remain firm and true.

I turned to Mary and gently said,
"Every young lady Nature determines she should take a mate,
She is endowed with beauty and sex, men cannot resist that trait.
When she has decided on the man she will wed,
She must make sure he will forever remain in her homestead.
Marriage is hard work, and it is the women folk who make it a success,
Keeping the husband happy and the children to bless.
Marriage is about partnership, teamwork and caring too,
Consider your loved one in everything you do.
Dad has been kind, loving, caring for us all,
Now he is giving you away in the church hall.
I am a woman, got my man and a happy family too,
My dearest daughter that is the best answer I can give you."

Stars in Your Eyes

Sherlock Holmes the world renowned detective
Issued his famous colleague Dr. Watson a directive,
To hire a tent and apparatus so they could go camping on Dartmoor.
Dr. Watson also organised appropriate clothing, which they wore.
On the site they pitched their tent and lit a fire,
Had supper, weary and tired they did retire.
In the dark of the night Sherlock woke Watson and said,
"Look up into the sky, tell me what you see, without getting out of bed."
Watson, surprised, looked up and mumbled, "A million stars and a beautiful
moon."
Holmes rapped out, "That's because they have stolen our tent, you buffoon."

The 3H Charity Shop

Hark, I hear the gentle close of a door
The 3H shop of Tunbridge Wells will soon be no more.
For twenty-five years it has been an asset of this society,
Accepting donated goods and selling with propriety.

The benefits and good will of this trading organisation
Will be sorely missed at its cessation.
Stalwarts of this charity shop gave their goodwill and benefaction
Giving their tremendous support, to ensure this successful operation.

The leading person for this success, it was plain to see
So much so she was awarded the MBE.
She now needs time to relax and enjoy some leisure
Supporting her family, grandchildren, giving her deserved pleasure.

All who know Enid Brown will salute her for her dedicated work
Come wind or rain her duty she did not shirk.
The shop was open to provide affordable goods to those in need,
And with her dedication and skilled management she did succeed.

Dear Enid, from all of us, we thank you yet again
Understanding your need to retire and release the strain.
Enjoy your retirement, which you truly merit
Your devoted work to the 3H Fund has earned you great credit.

This poem was written in appreciation to Enid Brown, who ran the 3H charity shop in Tunbridge Wells for twenty-five years, supported by the chairman, Albert Brown. She was awarded the MBE for her great effort in supporting the Help the Handicapped Holiday Fund, which provides holidays for the disabled and elderly.

Spring Is in the Air

When Mother Nature stirs from her Winter sleep
When the sun beams down his rays, warm and deep
When the days draw longer and lighter too
When azure skies turn the grey ocean a gentle blue.

When the chill winds of Winter fade and disappear
When gentle warm breezes arrive back here.
When bursting buds and Spring flowers show their face
When snow and ice are gone without a trace.

When birds sing with a mating note
When the animal kingdom sheds its Winter coat
When the pulse of life quickens each day
When the foliage of the World bursts forth, come what may.

When a young man's heart turns to love and romance
When the maiden leads her beau in a merry dance
When the farmer ploughs the field and sows the seed
When Nature stirs the earth for the World to feed.

When Spring revisits Earth on her annual spree
It is joyous and wonderful to be alive, healthy, well and free.

Who Is He?

Raise your glass to the man who is wisest and best,
Raise your glass to the man whose judgement passes the test.
Salute the man who is canny and bright,
Salute the man who sets your imagination alight.
Admire the man who gains your confidence with ease,
Admire his demeanour and out going attitude that all will please,
Cheer the man who is tall and strong,
Cheer the man who makes us feel we all belong,
Praise the man who can turn hatred into love,
Praise the man who can turn a tiger into a turtle dove,
Praise the man who can cure the sick and the ill,
Praise the man who can turn evil into goodwill.
Hail to the man who knows his own destiny,
Hail to the man whose verdict is as sound as sound can be,
He must be the man who is the spitting image of me!

I Want to Be There...

Where the willow dips into the river,
And nature's music fills the air,
When the sun is warm and benevolent,
Sitting at the water's edge, I want to be there.

Watching the swans glide by with gracious ease,
Ever together making a beautiful pair.
Watching the fish leap and snap the unsuspecting fly,
Sitting at the water's edge, I want to be there.

I look into the blue sky and see the billowing cloud,
Moving gently, brilliant white, reflecting the sun's glare.
The trees are green, beautiful in their summer dress,
Sitting at the water's edge, I want to be there.

The river runs deep, and ambles slowly along,
Its idle pace suggests it hasn't a care
An otter emerges from its den and gives me a stare
Sitting at the water's edge, I want to be there.

There is a time and place where I want to be
Alone, enjoying Mother Nature with its finery and life making me aware.
To relax and dream of all the wonderful things on our earth
Sitting at the water's edge, I want to be there.

Don't Give In

There are times when nothing goes right,
Seems no reason to stand up and fight.
Events and the world appear to be against you,
In despair, you don't know what to do.

Stop! Sit down, relax, evaluate your situation,
Study the for and against in your position.
The downs at first sight look heavy indeed,
Impossible to handle you will plead.

If the worst does happen, what will the outcome be?
Imagine you are there and try to see.
When disaster has struck and you are bereft,
Look around and see what you are left.

To face a new world, have you your health?
If so, this is vital to your future wealth.
If you have family and friends who love you dear,
This should dispel some of your present fear.

Think of the millions, handicapped and blind,
Racked in pain, driven out of their mind.
Those caught in the blood shed of war
No escape, always at death's door.

Think of the countless, living with starvation and drought,
Surviving each day with little or nought.
Those born into slavery, no day of rest,
For them God has not given of his best.

It will take time for these thoughts to digest.
Meanwhile hold the hands of those you love best,
Open your heart and let in those you adore,
Share your troubles, they will love you the more.

Look to the future, stand up and fight,
The world is good, you know that is right.
Every cloud, however dark, has a silver line,
Search hard for it, and you will do fine.

Your misfortunes at present liken to a tunnel without light,
Positive thinking will put your black despair to flight.
To you, it will never be the same again, But this world is a wonderful place,
Respond to it, and let it be your joy and solace.

NEVER NEVER QUIT
You owe it to yourself and family and friends,
They need you.

The Gate on Top of the Hill

When I was a young lad, my dad and I loved to walk in the countryside,
There were many lovely walks close to where I used to abide
On one ramble we came across a hill over looking the coastal shore,
It was a place I soon came to appreciate more and more.

On the brow of the hill was a fence and a gate,
Because of its commanding views, a bench was placed in state.
To those who could climb the hill and relax at the top,
One would sit and stare, mesmerised, a glance would become a long stop.

The coastline to the left stretched for many a mile,
Edged by tall cliffs, and rocks grouped in pile after pile.
One clambered over them to reach the pools with great care,
If the tide was incoming, only those with courage would dare.

The coastline to the right was blessed with beaches galore,
Our fore fathers had enjoyed its comforts centuries before,
Walking the soft sands in their bare feet,
Gentle waves washing them, another delightful treat.

Watching the incoming tide bring in the unfortunate shellfish,
To be picked up, to be cooked for the evening dish.
Seeing the crabs scuttle away as fast as they can go,
Realising the hungry beach walker was their foe.

Looking inland you could see our small town of Wicken hence,
It straddles the meandering river of the Ouse, from whence
It lazily runs down to the open sea,
Where it joins in the vivacious ocean spree.

In between the shore and the land around,
Green fields, hedges, fauna, such a variety of trees abound.
In the different seasons, come the changing views,
Grey of winter, green of summer, and autumnal hues.

When I was a teenager I did much courting up on the hill
Watching the sunset go down, would give us all a thrill.
Holding hands with your loved one sitting together on the bench,
Knowing when darkness falls, going home and parting will be a wrench.

When married we would take the family to the top of the hill,
To enjoy a picnic, play games in a setting so picturesque and tranquil
We would watch the horses galloping along the sands,
Bathers swimming, building castles in summer time, every thing was so grand.
Now my loved one and I are living alone,
Our family has grown up and flown,
We both struggle up to the top of the hill,
In the twilight of our lives Nature depicting until…?

Enjoy Today While You May

I arise from my bed and draw the curtain
To face a day, of which one is never certain.
What will happen to you or me
Whatever will happen, will be, will be.

I am fortunate to be alive on this earth
In spite of its troubles, its sorrow, its mirth.
I am fit, the key to life,
With it you can overcome trouble and strife.

I look out at the morning dawn
The world sings as another day is born
The heavens chaperone in the glorious sun
Its golden smile betraying warmth and fun.

Today I plan to walk over hill and down
To avoid the madding crowd and busy town.
Wishing to hear the babbling brook
To listen to the song of the mating rook.

To walk all day at a leisurely ramble
To ascend small hillock with gentle scramble.
To stop, listen and admire
To be part of natures great world out there.

I come to rest on the gentle seashore
Sit and appreciate the wildlife galore.
The birds in their flocks, a glorious sight,
Diving and searching for their daily diet.

Tired and content I am homeward bound
The night moves in without a sound.
'Tis time for me to think of bed
To lay down my weary and happy head.

To dream of a world as it should be
Where nature and civilisation live in harmony.
If we do not learn to live together
This world as we know it, will disappear forever.

The Sea

The sea is calm,
The sea looks blue and warm.
The enticed swimmer enters in,
To relax, enjoy and swim.
Undercurrents drag him down,
Death fits her fatal gown.
The sea is calm,
It beckons again with a smile.
Beware, the sea, the world
Is full of guile.

Di's Last Goodbye

I felt it was going to be our last goodbye
I sat by the hospital bed of my dear Dad Di.
He had reached the good age of seventy-nine,
Known for his generous smile—rarely did he whine.

He had a heart operation fifteen years ago
We thought we had lost him, but he wasn't prepared to go.
Whether it was through his stubbornness or he wasn't ready to meet his maker
That he survived the doctor said was a shaker.

Since then he has watched his diet, exercised every day
Took up short tennis, bowls and snooker did he play.
When Mum died he came to live with us,
He became an asset, not creating any fuss.

Our two sons really took to him,
He took them to football matches, on rambles and a weekly swim.
He encouraged them with their homework,
Nicely and firmly making sure they did not shirk.

His support meant my husband and I would enjoy some time of our own,
What was great the boys didn't mind or moan.
It gave Dad a new lease of life,
Kept him out of trouble and strife.

The last seven years he made himself part of our home,
As he got older he had less desire to roam.
He tried hard not to be a burden to anyone,
Was always ready for a joke, a laugh and fun.

Then it happened, disaster came, he crashed down the stairs,
On a loose carpet of which he was unaware.
He was rushed into hospital in a bad state,
The doctor saw no treatment could stop his fate.

He wouldn't survive a week or much more,
The first two days he recognised us and knew the score.
Then he lapsed into a coma and did not revive again,
Waiting for his demise was for all of us a strain.

It was Sunday at the hospital and the family were all there,
The doctor removed Dad's life support with care.
I held his hand and felt his life drain away,
It was best in his condition that he didn't prolong his stay.

I only wish we could have said our goodbye,
Yes, we were all tearful I cannot deny.
The nurse handed me an envelope and said
I was to give you this when he was dead.

The contents of the letter we put on his gravestone
Buried beside Mary so that he would not be alone.

I HAVE GONE TO JOIN MARY IN HEAVEN
THANK YOU ALL FOR YOUR LOVE AND CARE
DON'T BE SAD. I'M GLAD.
LOVE, GRANDAD

That was Di's last goodbye.

I Am in Love

I am walking on air, Peter adores me
That I love him too, it is plain to see,
I long to be with him day and night,
When we are together everything seems so right.
Many will say we are living in a romantic dream,
If so, to the paradise of love we will have been.
I am in love, I cannot say anything more.
I just want to be with the man I adore.
I am in love, I am in love, I am in love.

Your Smile

A smile costs so little, but is worth a great deal
It radiates happiness, encouragement, creates a good feel.
A smile cheers the weary and the tired,
Its boosts the loser, who wants to be admired.

Its provides much comfort at so little cost,
A smile attracts those who are alone or are lost,
A smile is a sign of a warm greeting,
The beginning of a pleasant meeting.

A smile up lifts the dispirited and the sad,
Seeing a smile makes them realise life is not all bad.
Smiles at home, the club, or in company.
Will generate friendship, love and harmony.

Smiles are more likely to dispel hatred and fear.
A grin would bring comfort to those to you are dear.
A smile to many is a happy blessing,
Straight from the heart without any dressing.

A smile enriches those who receive it,
It benefits those who radiate it.
A smile is natures way of bringing joy on earth
Which unfortunately there is a great dearth.

To everyone out there, I implore you all.
SMILE, SMILE, SMILE, let us all walk tall,
It's so easy to make this world a happier place,
Simply by presenting a happy and smiling face.

Enchantment

It has been a wonderful summer's day,
Coming to an end with the sunset in play.
It was a glorious ball of orange fire,
With a pink and blue sky, it was all you could desire.
My true love and I sat in the evening twilight,
Watching Mother Nature's beautiful and fading delight.
To encourage us to sleep, that we cannot forestall
Soon the darkness of the night would cover us all,
Hoping tomorrow will be another enjoyable day,
Occasions like this make the path of life such an enchanting way.

Our Stream

At the bottom of our garden runs a stream
On a summer's day idyllic to sit by and dream.
Basking in the sunshine, listening to its chatter
Dropping over the cascade with its cheery splatter.

When the stream arrived in our little homeland
Our predecessors its course had planned.
In its main route a waterfall was made
When bounding over its crystals on the rocks sprayed.

A sparkling waterfall is a joy to behold
Its freshness and cleanness more precious than gold.
Its vitality depends on its source and rain
After a shower watch its banks take the strain.

When planning its course a diversion was created
So that Nature's force and surge could be abated.
Into a pond it gurgles which has an island too
A little haven from Nature's point of view.

To sit quietly under the osiers by our lively rill
One relaxes and enjoys a gentle thrill.
Its closeness to Mother Earth one can always enjoy
Whether man, woman, girl or boy.

This natural wonder running through our patch
Is a gift not many today are blessed to match.
Listening and watching our stream on its cheerful way
Brightens one and all, even on the darkest day.

Lucky Me!

I will tell you straight I am not a religious man
But within reason I will help anybody when I can.
You can do that if you have your health
Some can do it if they have wealth.

What is wealth some wise men will say
Money doesn't ensure you will have a "Good Day."
Wealth can be your family, friends and loved one
Those who will mourn you when life is done.

There has always been misery, pain and joy since the World began
Much caused by natural disasters—more by man on man.
This very day so many nations, tribes, religions at war
Inflicting death, injury, terror instead of peaceful jaw-jaw.

With the world riddled with sickness and disease
Why mankind with wars create even more is a tease.
If only our womenfolk could make their warring men cease
And value the sweet harmony of life with the world at peace.

Every day I rise because I am well and able
Every day my family and I eat off a well filled table.
Every day we appreciate our quiet warm secure home
Every day we choose our pleasures and where to roam.

We value the privilege of having the right to vote
We value the fact that war in this country is remote.
We value our schools, our hospitals and police force too
We value our shops, leisure centres and our wonderful countryside in situ.

I am in the eventide of my fortuitous life
It has been paved with ups and downs, no terrible strife.
If there is a God, thank him, he has been kind to me
Making my span on earth, healthy, happy, enjoying peace and being free.

Oh lucky, lucky, me.

A Clever Woman

A clever woman is a woman who disguises the fact that she is clever,
A clever woman advises firmly and makes you feel you have made the decision.
A clever woman praises your achievements and covers up for your mistakes.
A clever woman always has a welcome mat and a warm heart.
A clever woman offers security and makes you feel independent.
A clever woman encourages enterprise, adventure and progress and offers you a
    safety net.
A clever woman gives a great deal and often receives little.
A clever woman gets satisfaction and joy in her wisdom and generosity.
A clever woman builds your confidence to face the big world outside.
A clever woman provides solace when disappointment and disaster strike.
A clever woman is a very important person in our society (often called Mum).

The Household Fly

I see a fly on the wall
I wonder why it doesn't fall
I see a fly on the window pane
Why it doesn't tumble down seems insane.
I see a fly on the kitchen door
It bewilders me why it doesn't fall down to the floor.
I see a fly stroll along our ceiling high
Surely it must topple down and die.
I see a fly buzz round and round at great speed
Why it doesn't crash into anything amazes me indeed.
Our common household fly has learnt to survive
Avoiding fly traps and pesticides in order to stay alive.
If disaster strikes and the human race meets its doom
I feel sure our able fly will still be buzzing round our room.

Heigh Ho—A Burglar Am I

Let me tell you I am a professional burglar as you see
I am only twenty-five, and am kept as busy as can be.
I pride myself as a dedicated and fair man
I rob lord or lady, the pensioner, the workingman, all with equal élan.

I vary my business hours working nights and often days,
Planning out my schedules according to the best pays.
Sometimes I survey a victim's movements over a period of time
Sometimes there is a pattern, others no reason or rhyme.

I specialise in stealing jewellery, plate, china and cash of course,
Any credit cards or passports I sell through another source.
Fortunately the public can be very careless indeed
Leaving windows and doors open, inviting me to succeed.

Of course I take a risk when I burgle a place
If I am caught what retribution do I face?
I must have done over one hundred jobs in the last year or two
If arrested I plan to confess and apologise for the last job I do.

I will be put on community service, so many hours to suit the crime!
When serving my penance it will give me plenty of time
To observe other prospects for burglary in my new capacity,
"I am doing my community service" I can say with audacity!

I prefer to work alone, it's safer by far
Sometimes I use a lookout who sits in my getaway car.
The newspapers tell you of the burglars who are caught,
They are so few it makes my risk virtually nought.

When my victim rings the police and informs them of a break in,
They issue the victim with a number for the insurance claim treating the matter
    as a minor sin.
They are too busy to visit the site and take fingerprints,
Catching burglars, giving them community service, the police fervour stints.

You may ask me if I am successful or not,
I will tell you at twenty-five years old what I have got.
Two days a week I live in my London tenement flat,
It is rundown, decrepit and full of tat.

From this den of iniquity I plan my robberies without fear,
The other days I live in my country cottage most dear.
I visit my yacht on the coast, and race my horse from a stable near.
Nothing registered in my true name that's very clear.

Adding up all my assets, including stocks and shares
They say a fortune comes to those who dare.
I could declare a total of eight hundred thousand or more
I could not have bettered that in any other profession I'm sure.

All burglars are grateful to our judges who seem to have no contact with real life
Never appreciating how burglars' victims suffer from trouble and strife.
I feel no remorse for those who experience my intrusion
When stealing their personal belongings, creating havoc and confusion.

Thank God the English law is an ass run by silly old fogies
Making heaven for burglars who become the victims' untouchable bogies.
The police only want to catch the speeding motorist
When caught, fine them and smack them on the wrist.

Remember, if my victim of robbery tries to defend
He has no right to strike me as he would intend.
To protect his home and possessions with forcible vigour
If he injures me I will sue him for a sizeable figure.

The Englishman's home is no longer his castle
Full of goodies, it can be opened as easily as a Christmas parcel.
Pick out the items you want of course and leave a mess
Think of the English legal system and our handicapped police force and I say
God Bless!

To conclude I will continue the profession I have chosen
On my ship of life I will be my own bosun.
It is tough for the injured and the wronged at the receiving end
However, no way my lifestyle to change do I intend.

HEIGH HO—A BURGLAR AM I

The Never Never Land

The stranger said, "Have you ever been to the land of "Never Never?"
I replied, "I am sure I haven't been there ever.
I thought you only went there if you were dead."
The stranger replied, "That myth by many it is said,
I admit most who go never want to come back,
Those who haven't been cry 'Alas alack,'
Come see where the Wango Wango Trees grow,
Where rivers of milk and honey flow.

Cows when milked produce marvellous malted whiskey,
That's why the farmers and the milkmaids are so frisky.
Elephants fly driven and guided by their spindly tail.
It's their ears that help them to sail.
It only rains when King Nod says so,
That's once a month, then everyone to church does go.
The temperature is always right, no cold, no sweat,
You can't borrow money, so no one is ever in debt.

Everyone has their own wings to fly around,
Most intelligent folk keep their feet on the ground.
Everyone sleeps from dusk to dawn,
You wake up feeling good, never time to yawn.
I have told you a few of the many things you will adore,
If you don't come now you will be forever sore.
You have only one invite, that is the law.
In Never Never land you will never be poor.

To refuse this wonderful opportunity you would be insane,
Because I will not be able to ask you again."
Tommy replied, "I would love to come, but I must ask Mum first,
To go without her permission I would be cursed.
Then I will come with you after I have had my tea."
The stranger smiled, vanished, back to the home of the free.
I knew then I would never go to the land of the "Never Never"
Not today, not tomorrow, or ever and ever.

Look at My Forehead

"George, the tap in the bathroom is leaking
Obviously it is a new washer it is seeking,
It's been like that for six months or more,
When are you going to repair it—what's the score."
George, Bett's husband, would always become irritated
When asked to do repairs or get the home decorated.

George snapped back, "Look at my forehead, I'm not a plumber
Find someone else with it to lumber."
"George, the small bedroom is tatty, needs to be decorated."
George again was obviously cross and frustrated.
Snapped back indicating he was feeling berated.
"Look at my forehead, I'm not a decorating man
Find someone else to do it, who, I don't care a damn."

"George, the steps on the front door need cementing and attention,
Getting them repaired now would be good accident prevention."
George now was really coming to the boil
On those doorsteps he wasn't going to toil.
"Bett, my dear, look at my forehead. I'm not a maintenance man."
Now so cross George went off to the local as quickly as a man can.

Many hours later George crawled back to his house
A little bit tipsy and awaiting him was his smiling spouse.
"George, you will be delighted to know I got those jobs done."
George couldn't believe his luck, it was like the rising of the sun.
"Well done, Bett, my love, how did you accomplish that?"
"When you left for the pub, I went out on the doorstep and sat.

"I cried my heart out and felt full of despair
Along came this handsome young man who said, "There, there,
What's troubling you, my love, you must not cry,
Is there anything I can do to help? I am willing to try."
"I told him of the jobs you would not do."
He smiled. "I can sort it out for you

There will be one condition I think that is only fair
Either you bake me a cake, or let me make love to you, if you dare!
When I have finished these jobs you can show your consent
And either of these conditions you can implement."
George said "What sort of cake did you prepare?"
"Dear George, look at my forehead, I'm not a baker, so there!"

My First Passion

It was one week after I was sixteen,
A long time ago that does seem.
I would meet my friends in the local park
Most Friday evenings in the summer for a chat and a lark.

The group broke up and Joe said he would walk me home
Not safe for girls to walk alone.
Before we got out of the park we sat on a seat
Quickly he gave me a kiss, I smiled, he became more upbeat.

With his hand round my waist he undid my blouse
Fondled my breast which my bra did house.
He put my hand down and told me to rub his thigh
I was getting warmed up—that I do not deny.

I felt a hard lump Joe told me to rub
A few minutes later we were both in the passion club.
We stood up and walked into the bush and shrub
We dropped to the floor, took off what was necessary, and continued to rub.

Five minutes later he entered me, I was excited as only one can be
After a while of pushing he stopped and smiled at me
Whispered, "That was good, did you enjoy it too?"
I replied, "It was good, but it wasn't worth such a to-do."

Joe said, "Next time we shall do it in a comfortable bed,
Work up our passions so we come together to a head.
I read a book which says it takes practice and time
To achieve the perfect act of making love desirable and fine."

I suppose as it was the first time I remember it well
That was ten years ago, tomorrow I will hear my wedding bell.
Since then I have had two lovers and have learnt so much,
Now I must settle down with my husband and caress him with my gentle touch.

I Love to Walk

I love to walk where few have walked before,
The quiet and lonely beach, with broken rocks, the ragged shore.
To view the sea, that's always in command,
It benefits Mother Nature and men's constant demand.
To amble along the freshly washed and virgin sand,
The sun smiling, the wind resting and gentle, isn't nature grand?
The gentle murmur of the distant waves is all one can hear.
A few hours later the incoming tide will appear.
The ocean is gentle, soothing, coaxing when Mother Nature is in good vein
When upset she hurls ferocious waves, thunderstorms and driving rain.
Not the time even with sou'wester to go walkabout
Safer to stay at home beside a glowing fire no doubt.

I love to walk where few have walked before,
In England's green and pleasant land that I adore.
The countryside in all seasons has much to be admired and seen,
In Spring the bold venture forth in faint sunshine, sharp air and temperature keen.
Wander through lanes where only evergreens add to the colour flow
In your experience and heart you know this isn't so.
You look for the young shoots bursting through the hardened earth
Fighting to be first and seen for all their worth.
In the front line with others thrust the snowdrops small and bright
After Winter's gloom they are a most welcome sight.
You admire the farmer's work in ploughed field and bustling farm
These fine yeomen of England husband their produce every year without qualm.

I love to walk where few have walked before,
Rambling, browsing in the Summer sun, who could ask for more.
The resurgence of Spring has clothed earth with leaf and flower
Now the Summer sun and rain will the Autumn harvest endow.
I follow the bubbling stream through wood and valley
On the river bank under shaded tree I reflect and dally.
White clouds reflect the sun's life giving light and beam
Enhancing the beauty of many a countryside's idyllic scene.
Now is the time for the animal kingdom to graze, eat and grow fat
Strolling through the leas and meadows give evidence of that
The joy of a gentle and pleasant summer passes much too soon
A benevolent summer to all the world is a cherished boon.

I love to walk where few have walked before
Visit the orchards where fruit ripens in quantities galore.
To wander round the cornfields of barley, rye and wheat
Standing side by side with root crops without which the harvest would not
be complete.
Stroll through the avenues of our beautiful trees
Sporting autumn colours with their tinted and shedding leaves.
The chill of the air is beginning to make its mark
The days draw in, the evenings lengthen and it quickly becomes dark.
The nostril picks up the smell and tang of bonfire smoke
Made by Guy Fawkes supporters and the garden fires of country folk.
On the ground one picks up the fruit of the chestnut and beech tree
In the lanes and by-ways wild berries to be picked range free.

I love to walk where few have walked before
Venturing into the cold winter climate, make sure you close the door.
The animals in their wisdom take their seasonal sleep
Others avoid the inclement weather and in their dens do keep.
The native birds now song less who remain in this country now cold and grey
Like us all sit out the winter waiting for the welcome spring day
When the snow falls and lies crisply on the ground
Stride out and see what winter treasures can be found
See the frozen pond glitter in the evening sun
Admire the children skate and slide, making their own fun.
Winter's here, enjoy it, the good and bad, come what may
At least we know it is not here to stay.

I love to walk where few have walked before
Whatever the time or season, I will find a scene that I will adore.
Mother Nature is truly beautiful, of that you can be sure
Respect her and she will in turn reward you evermore.

Three for the Price of Two (And Get One FREE)

Oh dear, what can the matter be
Look at the shopping trolley and you will see
The housewife does not buy one off anymore
After wandering around the superstore.

The buyer is enticed to buy three for the price of two
They say the third one is free—not true.
There is no such thing as a free dinner they say
If you have three for the price of two, you will surely pay.

Successful stores must be cost effective
Merchandise is sold, not at random or speculative.
Profit margins are set with great care
On all the goods that you eat, use or wear.

Competition is fierce to capture the customers heart
To encourage them with their money to part.
All the world loves a bargain we know
"Come to our store and see a great show."

Bargains galore will put your head in a spin
Not to buy must surely be a sin.
Marketing products is now a refined skill
Persuading the customer to ring up the till.

When you get home and reconcile the bill
How much you have bought, subtly against your will
How much you have bought, which you don't really need
Those extras are how much the stores succeed.

To all you customers I have this to say
Buy as you want, buy as you may
Be wary when you buy more than you need
Shop diligently and carefully and you will succeed.

HAVE A GREAT DAY!

A Baby Is Dying…

A baby in ward ten is dying, dying,
To save his life the doctors have stopped trying, trying.
The parents sit by his cot holding his tiny hand, crying, crying,
The baby in ward ten is dying, dying.

As sister of this ward dedicated to the care of the very young,
When lives are saved we smile with joy, when they die sorrow is sung.
My heart when we lose the fight is always wrung.
When we save a life, hats in the air are flung.

All the world celebrates when a new life is born,
To lose a babe, the world weeps and is forlorn.
Hearts of the deceased parents and kin are apart torn,
Another young soul will not face the following dawn.

The population of the world is growing, growing
More life than death Mother Nature on the earth is bestowing, bestowing,
The world moves forward and all life must keep flowing, flowing,
For the future of our earth we grope for, without truly knowing, knowing.

The baby in ward ten is dying, dying,
To save his life the doctors have stopped trying, trying.
The parents sit by his cot holding his tiny hand, crying, crying,
The baby in ward ten is dying, dying.

Stop and Stare

When we go walking—walking to anywhere
One of the joys of life is to stand and stare.
When you get to the very top of a hill
You stand and stare—oh what a thrill!

To look over the countryside—such glorious views
From the cliff tops scan the seas many hues.
Look down into valleys full of thriving trees
Swaying gently to the rhythm of the breeze.

Ready at dawn, viewing the brilliant ascending sun
Revelling in the glorious sunset when day is done.
Looking up to the skies in the dark of night
Watching in awe the stars twinkle with delight.

Stop and meditate in the quiet and splendour of a country wood
Hear the birds singing in harmony, so exhilarating—just so good.
Be still, listen to the rustle of the fallen leaves
Marvel at the animal kingdom moving with silent and stealthy ease.

To walk in this world is a privilege to nearly all
To stroll and enjoy our rich earth, answers nature's call.
Mother Nature is beautiful and bountiful as we are all aware
To truly appreciate all her wonders, surely we must stand and stare.

The Wind, Friend or Foe?

The waves roll in, the incoming tide is embracing the seashore.
A cool breeze, a warm sun, a setting we all adore.
We love to walk along the flat sandy beach.
Warm waters caressing our feet, what more could we beseech.

It only seemed a short time ago
That Mother Nature's mighty force did set her winds to blow.
This very spot was hit by a thunderous storm,
Mighty waves, a fearsome gale out of this tempest was born.

It blew down trees, and anything weak that stood in its way
Would not be left standing to see the light of another day.
Ships caught on the high seas knew this would be their last,
Their days were over of sailing before the mast.

The wind we cannot see but we can hear and feel.
All life before this mighty power must bow, and learn how to deal
With its ferocious energies, transporting rain clouds meeting the earth's needs,
Replenishing our rivers and lakes, without its water the Human Race would recede.

When the wind is constant, when the wind is strong,
She shapes rocks, cliffs, mountains with her compelling song.
In the Arctic and Polar lands the wind reigns supreme,
Every thing is deadly white, covered in snow, little sign of natures green.

The animal kingdom has learned to survive from this killer's cold knife,
Sleeping through winter, adapting quickly to preserve their precarious life.
The snow and ice formed in these glacial times,
In spring will melt and flow down to warmer climes.

The winds power has been harnessed to produce electricity,
This energy has created power for many a city.
Where mankind has stripped the earth of shrub and tree,
The wind has blown away the topsoil, leaving the desert to roam free.

The gentle winds blow the pollen and seed life around
Of our plant life, in order it can propagate and grow on fertile ground.
It purifies the air of man's polluted earth,
It sweeps and cleanses the world's entire girth.

I walk along the sandy shore, I look up into the sky,
The clouds look white and extremely high,
I debate with myself whether the wind is "Friend or Foe "
Without it, dear friend, we would all be in the land of long ago.

I Am in the Pink

"How are you today" my friends and neighbours frequently enquire,
"I am in the Pink" I respond with a grin as enthusiastic as a live wire.
I take so many pills I should be as fit as fit can be.
I take them periodically with a refreshing cup of tea.
My blood must be kept thin so I take daily my quota of warfarin
Every month I report to the clinic to see the shape I am in.

"I am in the Pink" compared to many others I know
When I wake up in the morning I know another day will flow.
I put in my false teeth, fit on my hearing aid so I can hear a lot more,
Place in my contact lenses otherwise my eyes would become very sore.
I am used to not having a good night's sleep,
I can't remember when last I had a repose that was long and deep.

"I am in the Pink" though my memory is failing, I always remember that clear,
I don't want folks to think I am a moaner, just a happy old dear.
Cry and you cry alone is an adage old and true,
I want my friends my companionship to pursue.
Old may be golden as they say, as long as you are not alone,
You need to be with friends and family, not abandoned at the end of a phone.

Yes, I have arthritis in my left elbow and knee,
Still with my zimmer I roam wild and free.
In my motorised wheelchair I often go on a shopping spree,
Or visit the local cinema, or go to friends for cake and tea.
They say be positive, enjoy each day as it comes, and that's what I think,
I want everyone to believe like me I am O.K. "I AM IN THE PINK."

The Boy Next Door

They moved in next door, I heard they had come from London,
Mrs. Brown was the mother, David was her 24-year-old son.
I thought he looked rather handsome, slim and tall,
He had a twinkle in his eye, a lovely smile as I recall.
We met on a Sunday morning looking over the garden wall,
He introduced himself in a manner to which any single girl could fall!
I did, hook line and sinker, there was no doubt,
My mother spotted it immediately, I was in love, there was no other shout.

She calmed down my excitement, told me to take it cool,
Pointed out David most probably had a young lady already swimming in his pool.
He mentioned at our first meet he was a mechanical engineer,
He had been promoted to office manager at a small factory very near here.
I had told David I was a secretary working in the local town hall,
Taking every thing into account it was a good safe job overall.
Then I did not see David for 6 weeks at least,
My mother said because I was frustrated I was acting like a beast.

David's responsibility was to progress the customer's contract
Inspect the work his engineers carried out, keep customer relations in good tact.
I knew if I wanted to catch his eye I would have to attract his attention,
To distract him from his new working situation which I had just mentioned.
One night when I knew he had come home late I paid him a call,
Asked him if he could help us to move a cupboard in our hall.
He like a gentleman came as I knew he would,
Helped us move this furniture as every gentleman should.

It gave him great pleasure in helping this lady and her mother in distress
He invited Mother and myself to tea on Sunday no less.
From that day on our friendship grew and grew stronger,
Until he realised our friendship was friendship no longer,
He had come to love me as I had always loved him so true.
He proposed to me, I accepted, What else could a girl do!
We planned to get married in 6 months time, in the spring,
When my mother heard of our engagement she made the following offering.

That David and I could live in her house and she would move out.
If agreeable she would move in with David's mother who agreed without any doubt.
David and I wondered how they would get on with each other,
They both affirmed there shouldn't be any bother.
Yes David and I got married and now have a family of four,
Our two boys have two adoring grandmothers living next door.
The only flaw in this arrangement is our boys are spoilt galore.
Otherwise I am so lucky to have married the boy next door!

Auntie Pat's Cat

Auntie Pat has had a cat for many a year
He is her companion, beloved pet she holds most dear.
His name is Tim, she keeps him sleek and fit
At 12 years old he is showing his age a bit.

She had Tim neutered to make him more docile
To detract him from spending courtships on the roof tile.
He has access to the garden through the cat flap,
Auntie doesn't know he ventures abroad through a garden gap.

Yes, Tim is Auntie's great love there is no doubt,
Anyone attempting to distract her attention in that direction would lose that bout.

She has made provision in her will should she die ahead
Of Tim, he will be provided for until he too is dead.
Then he is to be buried in the grave where Auntie does lay
Some will say this is true love going all the way.

I wonder if Tim's affection to Auntie is as great as hers to him
Not if Tim lets Auntie satisfy his every whim.
They say a pet's loyalty is to the hand that provides the food bin
They have a right to survive, that's no sin.
Auntie Pat needs someone to love, her pussy cat
To some giving care, getting love and affection back, life is as simple as that.

Six Feet Under

Yesterday we attended the funeral of our colleague Fred,
Over two hundred mourners came, some to see if he was truly dead.
Fifty years old is not an old age nowadays to die
But a shot in the head not even Fred could defy.

I am always amused when at a funeral a eulogy is read,
The tributes paid nearly always praise the dead.
I suppose it is to give comfort to their remaining loved ones what is said,
Knowing Fred's kinfolk, speak badly of him, you would join Fred.

Fred was his own man, never did an honest days work in his life,
Kept a trusted gang around him, including his devoted wife,
Paid others to take the risks, to steal, and he would keep the plunder,
Those who were disloyal in any way would feel his vicious thunder.

At the funeral Fred was praised for his kindness, generosity and charity,
All listening knew that these accolades were either rubbish or a rarity.
His son Joe will run our crooked organisation with a firm hand,
In the event of his demise Fred had all this planned.

I must be one of a few who knew how and why Fred died
We were in the act of robbing a bank, Fred had come along for the ride.
He was our lookout man, there to protect our backside.
The trouble was we were on another gangs patch
They got wind of our operation and were determined to prevent our snatch.

They crept up on Fred and with a silencer put a bullet in his head
When leaving the bank held us up, took the loot, sent us packing and instead
Of going home with loads of money which had always been our aim
One dead boss, outsmarted by another gang, result total shame.

As fate would have it our dead leader had made his biggest blunder
Paid the heaviest price and now he is six feet under.
Life goes on, we know his son is a bastard too
I wonder when someone gives his eulogy we will be told
"What a great guy he was for you."

The moral of this verse is plain to see
Eulogies are not always as truthful as they should be!

The Soldier's Drum

Rat a tat tat, the sound of the soldier's drum
What does it mean, the steady beat, the demanding *tum tum*.
Is it the call to war, to defend against the enemies threats
The war where the sun rises and for many never sets.
To those left behind, relatives, the wounded, some permanently maimed
War and death are impervious on whom their arrows are aimed.

Rat a tat tat, the sound of the soldier's drum
What does it mean, the steady beat, the demanding *tum tum*.
If you live in the fear of the oncoming enemy determined to destroy you
The *tum tum* of the drum will bring a fighting defence loyal and true.
Who will stand up and fight and keep the foe at bay
You pray and hope the *rat a tat tat* of the drum will with you stay.

Rat a tat tat, the sound of the soldier's drum
What does it mean, the steady beat, the demanding *tum tum*.
To the war widows and their families the drum beat will make them proud
Accompanied by sorrow that their beloved fathers and husbands now wear a shroud.
To them to hear the warriors drum beat sends a shiver down their spine
Glory in death brings them despair, poverty, recrimination in time.

Rat a tat tat, the sound of the soldiers drum
What does it mean, the steady beat, the demanding *tum tum*.
To the young warrior burning to fight for King, country and glory
The beating drums stir him to create a glorious victory.
Every nation must have these men willing to lay down their lives to fight.
To fight, believing their cause to defend you is the only right.

Rat a tat tat, the sound of the soldiers drum
What does it mean, the steady beat, the demanding *tum tum*.
The commanding drum with the nations warriors at its beck and call
Brings pride, inspires courage and respect before they in turn fall.
The strength and might of an army's heart responds to the drum beat
Dear God, preserve us all, give them victory and save us from defeat.

Mother Nature Speaks

Around our lake where we love to walk,
We hold hands, but do not talk.
The silence allows us to hear what Mother Nature has to say.
The mallards, Canadian geese and seagulls join in a squawking fray.

When they have settled and the quiet returns to us,
We are bemused and puzzled, not knowing the cause of all the fuss.
The stream that flows into the lake runs strong,
It gurgles over pebbles and rock and sings a lively song.

We hear the croak of frogs seeking a mate,
Mother Nature ensures they will get a date.
Buzzing bees collect nectar for their hives,
A warm summer, blooming flowers, ensures their swarm thrives.

We rest on the bank and admire the leaping fish
Snapping the river fly giving them a tasty dish.
During this tranquillity from their warrens rabbits appear,
As we sit still and silent they have no fear.

The sun informs us it is the closing of the day,
We rise, homeward bound on our way.
In the evening beside a glowing fire,
We reflect, it's been a good day, we are happy to retire.
We have enjoyed the sights and sounds of nature,
We pray mankind will respect them all and protect their future.

Along Came Ted

Evening is passing, night is coming fast,
Another long and lonely day is over at last.
Tom my husband died six months ago,
Time without him seems to move very slow.

I am fortunate to be healthy, comfortably settled in a house of mine,
Close by lives my daughter and family of three children divine.
I am always welcomed there, visit three or four times a week,
However it does not satisfy my persona so to speak.

I went to evening classes at the local night school,
Even tried swimming in the towns swimming pool,
I was restless, I could not find a friend in need,
I didn't know what I wanted, what advice to heed.

Then the clouds cleared, the sun shone, the sky became blue,
The answer to my malaise was soon to arrive on cue.
Going round the park on my evening stroll,
Whilst sitting on the park bench, beside the lake, a usual role.

Feeding the waterfowl from a bag of bread,
When sat down beside me a mature gentleman called Ted,
We started chatting together on that summer's eve
We got on so well, two lonely hearts getting over their grieve.

Ted suggested a future date, going on a coach trip together,
Getting to know each other regardless of the weather.
A week later two expectant people met at the designated coach stop,
It was to be a great day, for them it would not be forgot.

Our friendship grew stronger each time we did meet,
Three months later we both knew we shared the same heart beat.
I suggested Ted moved in with me for a trial run,
Ted said yes, but being married would be more fun.

I said I needed time to think his proposal through,
I thought of Tom, thirty years happily married together—what to do?
I spoke to my family for their views on this aspect,
They were firm, if Ted's proposal gave me happiness, then I should not reject.

When Tim died, he did not want you to die too,
He loved you, he would want you to enjoy the rest of your life, so do.
I married Ted a month later and am as happy as can be,
I am living life to the full and the future looks good for Ted and me.

I Feel So Tired

Oh dear what can the matter be, I do feel tired,
It seems only yesterday that all my spare energies were admired.
At sixty-five I should have a few years of get up and go,
But feeling as I do, this just isn't so.

However it has been explained to me the reason why?
The following statistics have astounded me I do not deny.
This country has a population of 58 million, that is on record,
26 million are retired leaving 32 million workers on board.

Data shows that 21 million are at school or university,
Leaving 11 million to work to their maximum capacity.
4 million are employed by the government, whose output is always low,
Their impact on the remaining workers encourages them to work slow.

We have 3 million social workers employed to look after you
Making sure with their bureaucracy you won't get what you are due.
On average there are 750,000 in hospital or permanently sick,
Another 250,000 nurses, doctors and ancillary staff to make the hospitals tick.

Half a million are banged up in a prison cell,
The unemployed, the lazy, the idle, or those feeling unwell,
Leaves a balance of two people fit and able left to do the work,
This places a huge responsibility on you and me that we must not shirk.
No wonder we both feel tired and washed out,
Carrying Great Britain on both our backs is the cause, no doubt.

Father Time Waits for No One

The church bells ring their message of joy,
Announcing the birth of a dear little boy.
Mother and child are both doing well,
Father thrilled to sire a son, this message the chimes tell.

Grandparents, uncles, aunts, and all other relations
Will pray on Sunday in church in celebrations
Proclaiming glory to God without reservation.
Newborn babes are the world's future and salvation.

That night the local doctor lost the fight
To save an elderly lady destined to share heavenly light.
Her death will mean the village will lose her goodness and charity,
She helped all when needed with her generosity.

Her funeral will be very well attended,
Nothing in her long life would she have amended,
Her appreciation was far and wide,
She had a kind word for all, that was not to be denied.

When the bell tolls for all who can hear,
This is the passing of a lady they hold most dear.
Life replaces her with a new born babe ready to start his day,
Whether he can compare with our lady only history will say.
All of us must die, our sperm will the future renew,
Father Time waits for no one, living or dying, all will be on cue.

Only One God

When I am asked what is my religion, I reply C of E,
Being Church of England gets out of explanatory repartee.
To the world I am not a church going man,
I tend to keep away from religious contact as far as I can.
I consider myself charitable, tolerant, considerate and kind,
Whatever your faith is, as long as it does not hurt others I don't mind.
You see I do believe in one god, only one god for this earth,
Who creates and controls my life from the instant of my birth.

Why does the world's population need so many different faiths to which they
    give their adoration?
Why are so many religions bigoted and show no toleration?
Because of different faiths wars are fought without cessation.
These religious wars create misery, inflict pain and total devastation.
I believe there must be one god alone, who created our wonderful earth,
Believing mankind would become civilised and prove his worth.
The world today is home to so many religious wars,
Whoever wins it never heals the terrible losses or the cause.

I have read it took seven days for God to create Heaven and Earth,
To many this theory is unacceptable and they respond with mirth.
"What came first the egg or the chicken" is the question I ask,
Religious leaders cannot answer and hide behind their priesthood mask.
God created the world and all life as only he can,
The strongest survived, especially cunning man.
It was the brain of man which enabled him to come out on top,
Now he is the most powerful living creature only he can stop.

Man is destroying himself with self-inflicted wars,
Greed and religion is usually the cause.
Man is depleting the seas, ravaging and raping our good earth
With his lust for power, mercy for life to him has no worth.
In a hundred years time I predict more or less,
This wonderful world of ours will become a wilderness.
Statues of false gods smiling down with distain,
Into empty cities, that will be all that will remain.

The one and only true God will be looking down from on high,
Appraising an empty wreck of a world which let its chance of happiness slip by.
The immortal creator of life will mourn the demise of the world, a tragic event,
Noting that man with his penchant for religious wars, peace and prosperity was
    never his intent.

What's Happened to the Train on Platform Four?

Over the speakers the reason given for the non departure and delay
"Leaves on line, workmen were working hard to clear the way."
The autumnal leaves are great when on a tree,
But when fallen, and at the mercy of the wind and blown free,
Combined with the seasonal rain and sticking to the railway line,
They become a menace as any engine driver will define.

At long last the track is cleared and the train is moving out of the station,
To the frustrated passengers it was a moment of quiet elation.
The nine thirty to Euston according to schedule was now an hour late
Moving at last was something to celebrate.
The steam engine chugged out of the terminus and picked up speed,
Its ovens burning fiercely the coal to satisfy avaricious need.

The expectant travellers who still have a long way to go
Heave a sigh of relief when they pass the cleared lines albeit slow.
For two hours their thunder horse progresses towards its London destination,
The mood of the passengers warming, digesting their previous frustration.
Suddenly the train slows and grinds to a standstill,
Another delay! Surely not! The passengers already have had their fill.

The passengers opened the carriage windows and put their heads out
Eager to learn what the latest delay was all about.
"Cows on line, men ahead are trying to clear the track"
The bovine grass eating marauders had broken through a fence and could not get back.
The grass on the banks of the sidings smelt fresh and green
That's what made the cattle hungry and keen.

A total of 22 had strayed onto the line,
Getting them back to their previous pastures so they could continue to dine.
This incident would add to this journey at least another hour
Making the passengers more discontent, certainly more sour.
The green flag waved, the engine was fired up and continued on its way
After thirty minutes the train stopped again for its longest stay.

The train pulled in at the village of Little Upnor
The engines stoker dashed to find the Station Master with the news he bore.
The engine driver was taken ill, had had a stroke
Needed urgent attention or he would soon croak.
The Station Master rang for an ambulance for instant aid
Emergency treatment was vital if his life was to be saved.

The Station Master rang for a replacement driver
The Stoker relaxed and took a well earned reviver.
Passengers were informed of this unexpected and pressing event
That it would take four hours to find and bring in a replacement.
The Station Master suggested that the passengers alighted the train,
Go visit Little Upnor to refresh themselves and revitalise their spirits again.

In the village pub "The Jolly Farmer" they provided good ale and beer
Together with a splendid menu which brought good cheer.
The local tea shop provided beverages, sandwiches and pastries of delight
Their jam tarts always tasty satisfying one's appetite.
The bakers shop sold rolls, cakes and sponges galore
When they ran out they simply baked some more.

The village church could to the troubled offer sanctity and peace
Where one could pray for all problems to cease.
One hundred and sixty visitors moved into Little Upnor to the delight of the catering trade.
Taking advantage of this unexpected windfall of business must be made.
Four hours later the passengers were all aboard praying that their iron horse
Would be moving soon to finish its designated course.

The new engine driver signalled that all was ready to go
He had been briefed of the passenger's frustration and that was all he needed to know.
He took the train to Euston, this time without any bother
At long last this exasperating journey was over
An announcement through the station's loud speakers was loud and clear
Obviously meant for all and sundry to hear.

"THE TRAIN COMING IN AT PLATFORM 4 IS EIGHT HOURS LATE
WE APOLOGISE TO THE PASSENGERS AND THOSE INCONVENIENCED
   BY THIS STATE.
DUE TO LEAVES ON LINE, COWS ON TRACK, A SEVERE HEART
   ATTACK
WE WERE UNABLE TO PREVENT THIS TRIPLE SETBACK."

Sweet Sixteen

She was a teenager about sixteen I would say
Passed my office window twice a day.
She has long dark hair and a lovely smile,
With her pleasant manner most she would beguile.

Her figure is one all men would admire,
It would fill her lover with passions of fire.
Her blue eyes, red lips, fresh face devoid of paint,
Because she doesn't need to be what she ain't!

Her lovely legs exposed by her short skirt
As she gently sways past, puts the males on the alert.
When she matures and unfolds her feminine charm,
Men will be captivated, fearing no harm.

I wonder if she will marry a young man for love,
Or become an older gentle man's turtle dove.
Who ever she marries in her future life,
I hope her husband like me ends up with a wonderful wife.

White Horses

I walk along the beach watching the incoming tide,
Combined with a strong wind they will not be denied
The white horses ride proud on many a wave
Gloriously white, foaming and how devilishly they behave.

On the rocky shores they mercilessly crush everything in their way
Sinking boats and ships that now on the sea bottom lay.
They are a force of Mother Nature man cannot withstand
So many times the white horses have wrecked what man has built and planned.

I see the young folk on a bright summer's day
Challenging these white horses with their fine wind-surfing display.
The surfers ride high, twirl and spin and enjoy their way
But it is the white horses that reign supreme and will always have their final say.

Jodrik the Brave

Boom, boom, boom the cannons roared
Boom, boom, boom the cannon balls soared
They smashed into the defenders barricade
Great holes in their defences were made.
Boom, boom, boom the cannons roar again
Death and destruction is their pitiless refrain.
Now in a parlous state the city of Triege
For a month it has been under siege.

Boom, boom, boom the last fusillade of the day
Tomorrow the besiegers plan to have their sway.
President Herlot with his army is enforcing his will
Those who do not obey him he will kill.
The Mayor of Triege knew this desperate city must make its last stand
Called an urgent meeting to see what defence could be planned.
All agreed that unless the six terrible cannon can be knocked out
The future for them all is lost without doubt.

They have one night to repair the battered barricade
To silence the guns or all hope will fade.
The Mayor stated that they could not muster a force strong enough
To charge the cannons, it would only receive a fatal rebuff.
The meeting sat silent, full of despair and remorse
Until a captain of the guard said, "We cannot beat them with our force
But if we can silence the guns I know we can defend our walls of course.
I have a plan which I need you all to endorse."

"My sixteen-year-old son who knows guns well and is brave
Is prepared to risk his life for the city to save.
He will steal out of our city in the dark of tonight
Smuggle through the enemy lines, keeping well out of sight.
The cannons will be unguarded, the guards in repose
They have no reason to fear what the evening could dispose.
On reaching the cannon all standing in a row
Placing gunpowder and cord in each barrel in a fashion so

When ignited all six will be detonated at a single blow
To ensure the success a huge distraction must be put on show."

"At two in the dead of night we must put on a firework display
To make the enemy wonder and marvel at our array.
At the same time Jodrik will break through the enemy line
Carrying out the operation as we would define.
When he hears and sees the city's explosive display
He will light the fuse to blow the cannon away.
He will have three minutes before the guns explode and so
In that time he must get away as far as he can go."

The Mayor sighed deeply and said, "Thank you for your bravery
What else if the city is not to fall to Herlot's slavery."
With little time left the plot was put to plan
A prayer went out with Jodrik from every child, woman and man.
Five minutes after the city's fireworks began
Jodrik lit the fuses, making his escape as quickly as he can.
What had not been calculated was that the cannons were next to the ammunition store
The explosion of the guns detonated the arsenal and slaughtered half Herlot's army
    and more.

Morning dawn exposed the chaos and carnage for all to see
That morning the besiegers rode out and delivered no mercy.
The soldiery and citizens of Triege searched the battlefield
For Jodrik their hero, their saviour, but his body it would not yield.
Their joy and relief of victory of having their city saved
From an evil enemy dominant, wicked and depraved.
Was diminished when they thought of Jodrik now passed away
His heroic bravery would be remembered many a day.

The citizens of Triege erected a monument
Of Jodrik depicting his total involvement
Of his self-sacrifice in saving the city of Triege
From the invader Herlot and releasing them from his terrible siege.

Together

I hear the clock ticking, the keeper of time,
I wait impatiently to hear the seven o' clock chime,
When it sounds I arise and put on my coat,
To respond to the letter my girl friend wrote.

Yesterday I received a letter in the post
From Jennie who I love most.
She has been away for a month or more,
She is the lass I do so adore.

She is coming home on the evening train,
Her absence has been a strain.
I look in the mirror, see my hair is parted right,
Put on a big smile, I want to be a welcoming sight.

I go out to the car, check the flowers in the back,
My enthusiasm to welcome her does not slack.
I have arranged to take her out to a dinner tonight,
All will be happy, warm and bright.

At the station the train steams in,
The train is packed, I don't see her till the crowd does thin.
We run to each other, she drops her case to the floor,
In my arms once again I have the girl I adore.

The Homecoming

I have returned to England from the land of the didgeridoo
The land of the kangaroo, and there are quite a few.
For forty years I have lived in the Aussie outback
Rearing sheep, shearing the wool off their back.

For the first ten years our home was a wooden shack
Every amenity, especially water, we did lack.
All my life my favourite colour was green,
In this part of the world it was rarely seen.

For my dear wife Edna life was a long chore
What kept her going was our son Tom whom we both did adore.
He was educated sixty miles away
He boarded at the schools, at weekends he came home to stay.

Then he won a university scholarship in biology
It meant he would go to England to continue his study.
There he achieved his degrees, a fellowship, and a loving wife
He became successful, had a family, enjoyed life.

We missed him as any parent would
He had his own life to make we clearly understood.
A few months ago Edna suddenly became very sick
We quickly got her into hospital, but that didn't do the trick.

She passed away in a deep sleep with little or no pain
Losing my love there was no reason to remain,
Alone in the outback, my neighbour the desert plain
Then I heard the most welcome refrain.

Tom and family offered me a home with them and retire
I gladly accepted, to return to England was always my desire.
I am now 74, have family love, share a warm home
Till my days run out I shall not be alone.
My homecoming will only be truly complete
When Edna and I sit together again on our divine seat.

Jill's Sick!

The editor sat in his office working away,
Jill his secretary her typewriter did flay.
His phone rings. "Oh God not another."
It turns out to be Jill's mother.

"I am just ringing to tell you Jill has a cold,
So she will not be in today" was the story she told.
The editor was surprised and said, "That's queer,
Jill's in the office now full of vitality and cheer."

"Oh," said Jill's Mother, "I must have got the date wrong,
It's tomorrow she will be poorly and not very strong.
Forgive me for getting the dates muddled,
Trouble when getting old you easily get befuddled.
Still it is nice to know in advance
Tomorrow Jill won't be working, instead enjoying herself in France."

Noisy Pups

Two noisy pups began to fight,
In their basket in the middle of the night,
Dad came down to see what it was all about,
It was over an old bone there was not any doubt.

He took it away, threw it into the dustbin,
But this didn't stop the pups making a din.
So he picked up the pups and put them outside on the garden floor,
He left them outside, it began to drizzle, he shut the door.

Two minutes later they were crying to come in,
To leave them out any longer would be a sin.
Dad towelled them down and let them know,
Any more noise then back into the garden they go.

They clambered back into their basket and soon fell asleep.
Through out that night there wasn't another peep!

Howzat!

It was glorious weather, the cricket match was soon to begin
To waste this lovely sunshine would be a sin.
There is some information to you I must impart
Before this battle of bat and ball is to start.
The opening batsman is the umpire's son
In front of his home crowd he wants to make his first ton.

The opening bowler is Freddie Truman of England fame
His reputation for fast bowling the cricketing fraternity do acclaim.
The scene is set, the batsman takes his guard
Batting against Fiery Freddie will be hard.
Freddie raring to go, runs thirty yards and bowls at the wicket
Batsman plays forward, misjudges, and snicks it.

First slip takes a good catch, the result is not in doubt
Freddie looks at the umpire and gives a thunderous shout.
The umpire shakes his head and says, "Not out—Not out."
Freddie picks up the ball and bowls again
The batsman plays forward—plumb LBW—"Howzat" is everyone's refrain.
The umpire stands impassive—he is not giving his son out.
Negatively shakes his head—element of doubt?

Freddie's temper was now beginning to run very high
He walked back with the ball for another try.
This time he sent down an absolute corker
It was an unplayable inswinging yorker.
It knocked the three stumps out of the ground
Triumphantly Freddie waved his fist in the air and turned around
And said to the umpire without being verbose
"By gum, lad, that must have been close!"

Marriage the Old Fashioned Way

We were all born in the town of Innispree
My three sisters, Mum, Dad and me.
We lived in an age when a girl's future was to be wed
Marry the right man if you want to get ahead.
Rearing four girls and a mortgage too
Dad had his work cut out, that was true.
But it was Mum who groomed us for our future destiny
To attract Mr. Right, marry and have a family.

Mum was industrious and always cheerful
To be lazy and negative she would regard as dreadful.
In our home we all learnt how to cook
Good food always kept a man on the hook.
To organise, be tidy and make a warm home
Make your man feel wanted and you won't be alone.
On our kitchen wall in a prominent place
Was a picture of Auntie with a huge smile on her face.

It was to remind us to smile, smile, smile
An important step if a man you wanted to beguile.
We had twelve records and a record player
Dad taught us to dance, smile and be gayer
Than the other girls on the dance floor
Making the young man want to walk you home to your front door.
Mum made us dress as feminine as can be
She said with our smiles and charm no chance had he.

The young man thought he was making the running
Didn't realise it was the lady who was doing the gunning.
When we reached sixteen or just over
Mum gave each of us her view of sex and the masculine rover.
We all realised that to have a child out of wedlock
Future happily married life would be put on the block.
Sex was taboo before the great day
However hard the ardent lover wanted his way.

She didn't mention that we might want it too
Still it was the woman who took the risk, so it was up to you.
All our lives my sisters and I were primed to get married and mate
Better than being a spinster with a job third-rate.
So it came to pass that my sisters and I married one, two, three and four
We all married well, who could ask for anything more.
Yes, we are happy with children to adore
When one is alone you think is there anything more?

For women who want to work, travel and politicise
Create their own futures and their rights to exercise
I know the world is slowly turning that way
When women will become leaders and hold their sway
I wish them well and will support them too
Their prominence in the world is long overdue.
My sisters and I are happy with the way our lives have been set
With our loving families we have no regret.

Surprise, Surprise!

John and Jean had both reached retirement age
They lived close to the seaside so they could engage
Walking in the country and particularly along the seashore,
The variation of tides, sea birds, weather, the sea walk was never a bore.
One sunny afternoon walking on the pebble beach
They came across a green bottle stuck in a rocky niche.

John picked it up and carefully pulled the cork out
From the bottle flowed green smoke, about
Six feet high and four feet wide
Out of it stepped a genie who was not to be denied.
His joy of being free again and breathing fresh air
He turned to the amazed couple and spoke slowly and with care.

"You can appreciate I now hold my freedom most dear
You have no reason of me to fear.
Any wish each of you want or desire
I will endeavour to fulfil."
The genie turned to Jean and spoke
"Give me your wish so your satisfaction I can invoke."

Still stunned she uttered, "Please put a million pounds in my banks
Do that, and it will be me giving you unreserved thanks."
The genie waved his wand and said, "It is done.
I hope this money will bring you great happiness and fun."
Turning to John he said "It is your request I now ask.
Satisfying it will be my happy task."

John quietly said, "I would like my wife to be thirty years younger than me."
The genie replied, "If that is your wish then so it shall be."
The genie waved his wand and touched John to see if he was still alive.
John sat motionless on the beach blinking, not believing he was now ninety-five!

Goddess of Love

O Venus, Goddess of Love I thank thee
For guiding an Adonis to find and love me.
He has uplifted my spirit, I feel so free,
In this wonderful world I feel so happy.

To us our love is a beautiful bond,
Every day our touching and caressing makes us grow more fond.
His closeness to me makes sadness and misery abscond,
His love and adoration for me shines like a diamond.

O Venus, Goddess of Fertility I thank thee,
Gracing me with motherhood and my love's desired paternity.
The future looks wonderful with our great love and coming family,
With your support we shall be as content as content can be.

Our life in this world is not very long,
Dear Venus on this earth your presence and kindness is strong,
Your endearments encourage us to sing worldwide a happy song,
Under your auspices you unite us all into a thriving ménage of which we all belong.

Who is in Charge?

The macho male and ego has his will
Since the world began and has still.
The alluring female lets him think what he may,
But she is the one who gets her way.

The male is physically stronger than the lass,
Her lithesome figure and feminine guile overcome the difference in mass.
The male can outrun his female counterpart,
Her demureness and femininity will win his heart.

The man is dedicated to provide for the family.
It's the woman who provides the love and stability.
The desire of woman and man for each other
Ensures they will mate and produce another.

It is important that the family will live in harmony
So that the human race can continue its future destiny.
It's the woman who tempers man's fire,
It's the woman who lets him think he is the sire.

It's the women folk often in the background,
Ensure the future of the world is sound.
Men's ambition and drive incur many a war.
It's the women who shoulder the misery caused and
Wonder what it was all for

Perhaps the world would enjoy more peace
And confrontation and conflict would cease
If our ladies ruled this earth
And all our efforts contributed to happiness and all its worth.

Some would say if this happened women would become like men,
Making enemies they seek to confront, and go to war again.
Dear Lord, if that be so, will the world ever be at peace,
When love and happiness prosper, and wars forever would cease.

Why?

It was ten years ago to this very day
Lee, my husband, was hit by a car and passed away.
He would have been sixty if he had been alive,
He had plans for both of us, if as expected, he did survive.

The mortgage was paid off last year,
We had no other debts to fear,
We had a fair-sized inheritance that made our day
Lee was going to retire early on his sixtieth birthday.

We had planned to go on a three month round the world trip,
By way of a cruise on a first class ship.
We had worked hard to bring up our family of four,
Now they were settled we anticipated having our own front door.

When Lee and I married thirty-five years ago,
Our great love for each other did show.
Bringing up our family had its ups and downs,
We enjoyed great happiness and occasional frowns.

Dear Lee, today I visit your grave and lay my flowers,
I go with good heart remembering our many happy hours.
Tomorrow I shall walk through the countryside, enjoying the flowers and trees,
I will remember your love embracing me like a warm summer breeze.
I will remember your smile, kind and generous heart,
Dear Lee, the world was good to us—why did we have to part?

She Pulls the Strings!

Most ladies Mother Nature has decreed will get their man,
Most ladies with that in mind will do all they can.
They are blessed with sex, femininity and female charm,
Mother Nature ensures man is seduced without harm.

The predatory female will raise the man's passion and fire,
With her attributes of womanhood and beguiling desire,
She will smile, cajole and praise him to the limit,
The man has no chance, and will to her submit.

Become the lady's lover and husband too,
Because Mother Nature wants a family to ensue.
This cycle for the lady does not end here,
Man has a roving eye, so ladies take care.

There's always another woman who would attract him to her lair,
She too will use the art of feminism to entice him, so take care.
Once you have got your man, the new game has started
Keep him happy everywhere if you don't want to be parted.
Make sure in the home he feels like a king,
Make sure in the home it is you the Queen who pulls the string.

Freddie the Mouse

In darkest midnight Freddie Mouse would pop out of his hole,
To look for kitchen titbits was his goal.
His best bet was to raid the kitchen larder,
If the door was slammed shut it would be harder.

He would have to climb up through the air vent,
Over the door, that would be his intent.
When inside, usually twice a week, no more,
He didn't want cook to realise he was snitching from her store.

He nibbled the cheese, only the crumbs and the odd off cut,
Ate the bread scraps, didn't touch the but,
He could smell the ham strung up high,
To go for that was too risky to try.

If the top was off he would jump into the vegetable basket,
On Tuesdays and Fridays it would be fresh from the market.
He loved young carrots, those he did adore,
Eating them completely, leaving no evidence to be sure.

Occasionally from the milk jug he could lap.
Otherwise he would drink from the dripping water tap.
He had been coming to this pantry for nearly a year,
Following in the footsteps of his mother most dear.

It was here she died in a mouse trap,
Knowing this he avoided repeating this mishap.
The snare and bait was always placed on the floor,
The safe way in was always the vent over the door.

Tomorrow he would feed outside in the garden and wood,
Searching for insects and seeds as mice should.
He had learnt how to grub and wait patiently for his prey,
He was an opportunist and tackled most that came his way.

Now he would cautiously wend his weary way,
Back to his nest in the skirting board to sleep and stay.
Rest contented until the dawn does come,
Then seeking his next meal in the light and sun.

How Mary Got Her Man

I was widowed five years ago, married for twenty years in fact,
Bill my departed was a good husband in every tract.
Though retired, he was active and passionate too,
I have always enjoyed my love life, without it I feel blue.
In the last year I have dieted and got my weight down,
I can now slip into many an attractive gown.
With the support of the right bra, my breasts are an attractive sight.
Yes I am looking for another man, and intend to put up a good fight.

When I did my light exercises down at the gym,
I could not spot or attract a married or unattached him.
I have persuaded Joan to think along the lines I do,
And to see if we can hook a man who is keen and true.
We spent three weeks on holiday together in Benidorm,
Yes we found some passion, then our lovers left us, leaving us forlorn.
Still we were encouraged, so when we got back home,
We knew we would have to find another dog to chew a different bone.

We decided to try the dating game.
It meant we parted company, it didn't seem the same.
We worked hard for three months, kept all our appointments and yet
Being on our best behaviour, full of feminine charm we just didn't get
A man who could satisfy us, amuse us and was good company,
Confident he would love us, be gentle and full of sympathy.
Life is full of surprises and then I had an unexpected one,
Because of my amorous activities my garden had lacked attention.

I advertised in the local press and got one reply.
I was fascinated by his voice on the telephone I do not deny.
Peter was aged fifty-five and turned up to see the garden and me
Thursday afternoons was the only time he was free.
He wasn't bad looking, was quiet, had a lovely smile
I was taken to him, him I was going to beguile.
His first Thursday he had a lot of work to do and clear
The weeds, mow the lawn, drain the pond and make it appear
More like the pleasant garden it used to be.
His effort and experience was there for all to see.

When he had finished around six I invited him for tea,
Which to my surprise he accepted gladly.
He went to the bathroom and I told him to take a shower
I knew then I wanted to capture him with all my power.
I listened through the bathroom door and heard him drying
I knew he would be naked without even trying.
I stepped into the bathroom in my sauciest underwear
Kissed him, caressed him and invited him to my bedroom if he dare.

Minutes later we were both in my bed
In this short time all our inhibitions had fled.
Yes, we made love with heated passion
After an hour we both relaxed with great satisfaction.
Then he said to me, "I really must go, my mother is ill.
If I could take you to lunch on Sunday that would give me another thrill."
On Saturday morning I was delivered a bunch of flowers
With a little note stating he couldn't abide the waiting hours.

To meet me again the following day,
I had a wonderful feeling I was on my way.
After lunch on Sunday we went to the park for a walk
Holding hands then we sat on a bench for happy talk.
The next few months we met three times a week
Going out, making love, enjoying each other so to speak.
Then Peter's mother died, I sat beside him while he cried
She was eighty-nine, poorly, the inevitable was not to be denied.

A month later when we were enjoying a dinner cooked by him
He proposed to me, if he hadn't I would have proposed to him.
This afternoon we shall be married when the church clock strikes three
I feel so happy, as happy as one can be.
The moral of my story you may or may not agree
If you want a mate, or just give up your virginity,
If you sit at home waiting for Mr. Right to knock on your door
You could be waiting for a long, long time to be sure, to be sure.

Get on your horse and go looking for your man
And when you make contact follow your plan.
With your female charms, and with your sexual attractions too
You will entice him into your adoring arms—will that do.
No way do you have to be the lady sitting at the back
Get on your horse and lead the attack.
Good Luck and Good Hunting.

The Winter Through

The month of October has this year completed its stay,
The Autumn leaves in the blustering wind swirl, dance and play.
The rain dampens their spirit and they settle down
Eventually nature dictates they will fertilise the ground.
The dark nights of November now descend very quick
Seasonal bonfires headed by Halloween, Guy Fawkes, witches and old Nick
Burn harvest debris, old bushes, aged brambles, thereby cleansing the land.
Putting our precious earth to sleep, giving it an encouraging hand.

Jack Frost is now a regular visitor with his spiky finger
Making the morning chill, colder, with tendencies to linger
They say he kills off insects and other pests
For that alone the farmers welcome him with zest.
Now November sleeps again and will not waken for another year
December arrives with wind and rain and will depart after the Xmas cheer.
The days are short, the nights are dark and long
We keep our spirits up with candle light, roaring fires and a cheerful song.

The Winter months of this year are now over at last
When the Yule tide signals the dreary month of December is past.
January rolls in with the babe of New Year in its arms
Winter's heavy weather is still with us, have no qualms.
On better days the sun peeks through the overhanging and dull cloud
Jack Frost's continuing presence ensures forgetting Winter is not allowed.
It is January that usually heralds in romantic snow
It is pretty and white—a result of the north wind's blow.

February claims her place in the Winter entourage
Her gift is to provide storms both small and large.
The farmer now sows his seed for this year's harvest
And prays his results will be fruitful for the effort he has to invest.
March winds blow and rain torments us all
The first signs of Spring make us feel good, walk tall.
The bursting buds on the trees, snowdrops displaying their beautiful face
The world is beginning to feel a better place.

Mother Nature is beginning to shed her Winter coat
All life on earth is responding and taking note.
The days are brighter, longer and the sun shines more
Spring is on the way, this is the time we all adore.

The Spring of Life

What keeps this sceptred isle of ours so lush and green,
Where an arid desert is so rarely seen.
We know it is the water running in the streams, rivers, lakes and meres,
Starting as trickling streams, becoming torrents running over cascades and weirs.

Underground wells spread throughout our green and pleasant land
Filled by the rain supplied by Nature's hand.
The springs rise and start their often long and exciting way
Other springs and sources join it and make their play.

The stream is growing and growing and turning into a small river
Its waters are vital becoming one of Nature's life-giver.
As it gently flows through the countryside
Villages, towns and cities develop on its banks and reside.

If its final destination is the meeting of the sea
Its waters will be absorbed in the ocean's melee.
What keeps this sceptred isle so lush and green?
Since the World began the springs have supplied water pure and clean.

In far away lands natives often do not know if there will be any water today
Their lives depend on the little water that may come their way.
When the rain falls don't moan and groan and despair
Without it our green and pleasant land wouldn't be there.

The Wonder of Music

It is around you, it surrounds you, it is everywhere,
It comforts you, it inspires you, consoles you, keeps you from despair.
Musical melodies make the world go round,
It is in the heart of every nation, its intrusion is profound.

Much music has a religious back ground,
In ancient and modern rituals and ceremonies music will be found.
As the human race became more civilised and mature
Music entered our lives more and more, our hearts and minds to secure.

The sound of music comes in numerous variations
Written in different tempo and depth to suit all taste and situations.
From the robust, the jazzy, the beat of marching bands, the trumpet voluntary,
Orchestra's playing classics, the pianist playing solitary.

Songs of praise, love, passion, songs of war
There is music to fit any mood, some you hate, most you will adore.
Choirs sing their hearts out with joy, providing audiences with entertainment,
Musicians are encouraged with awards to reach higher attainment.

Why is music so important to the human race, one and all,
To the warriors and defenders of our country it can be their clarion call.
The harmony of music helps us to relieve our stress,
Uplifts our spirits and reduces our distress.

Music can be inspirational, drive our ego and motivation,
Be our companion at home, or accompanying us to a far away destination.
You cannot imagine this world without music and its harmony,
That all the world embraces it, adores it, is its own testimony.
Music makes the world a better place, that I can truly quote,
We can sing its praises evermore, but now I finish on this high note!

A Time to Sleep

It is time to go to bed
To lie down and rest your weary head.
It has been a long day and you are weary
The weather has been awful and you feel dreary.

You have done all the jobs that need attention
Plenty more you are not going to mention.
It is time to turn off the light and close the door
Get into bed and sleep, that's what a bed is for.

To slip into sleep and hopefully dream
Of where you would like to go to a distant exotic scene.
You meet past friends and make many more new
Taste wines and foods of which you never knew.

And when you waken in the morning feeling fresh and bright
After enjoying a most comfortable night
Eager to start another new day
Your spirits rekindled to take on come what may.
They say life is what you make it that is true
It certainly helps when you have had a good night's sleep behind you.

Good Old Bill

Bill was seventy two active and retired,
Born with a deformed hand that was not always admired.
Bill had always been looking for things to do, any part time work,
Living alone, it kept him busy, meeting folk was an extra perk.
Unfortunately with his problem hand and grey hair,
Work opportunities for Bill were rare,
When prospective employers interviewed our Bill,
They sent him away saying, "Sorry, mate, but you are over the hill."

Bill's hobby was walking in spite of the weather,
He loved the rivers, the trees, the lowlands, the highlands and its heather.
He loved the Lake District, and walked there when he could.
There he felt comfortable, at home, he felt good.
Now he was bored, though it was November he was determined to go,
He knew that time of the year one could get a blizzard or snow.
He left the hostel at the first break of light,
Making the most of a short day he felt was right.

Bill took with him. his stick and mobile phone, a torch and dressed in warm gear.
The skies looked clear from that aspect he had nothing to fear.
In his knapsack, food and drink to see him through the day.
He had planned to be back at the hostel before nightfall if he had his way.
At three in the afternoon he was walking along a cliff quite high,
Homeward bound when he did espy
Two bodies lying in a crumpled heap,
At the bottom of a cliff most steep.

He worked his way down to the victims as quickly as he could
His heart beating, trying to work out a plan as he should.
He had to establish whether they were alive or dead,
If alive, ring emergency services, the first thought in his head.
He examined the bodies, both were injured, but alive,
What to do till help does arrive?
He got through to the emergency services, they told him what to do,
Keep them warm, give them drinks, keep their spirits high,
Don't let them sleep or they might die.

The rain started to pour down and strong winds blew.
He had to act quickly that he knew.
He gently pulled the injured into a cave,
To keep them dry and their heat to save.
He found bracken and wood and lit a fire,
Hoping to provide light and more heat in this situation most dire.
He built the fire to make it a beacon.
With straws he gave them a drink and told them to reckon
Help would be there within the hour,
A rescue team was coming in a helicopter for the area to scour.

To establish their where about and bring the medical aid and power
They were coming as quickly as they could to their rescue,
Only bad weather could delay and make them overdue.
Into the pouring rain, the driving wind, Bill left the cave,
He was determined these two men he would save.
He climbed the cliff to the very top,
And waved and waved his torch, he would not stop.

He heard the sound of the helicopter, it seemed far away
He muttered, "Please, please, Dear Lord, may they come this way"
The pilot saw his torch flashing and saw the fire,
He landed cautiously in case he too became a funeral pyre.
The rescue team jumped out and ran into the cave,
They were in time for the injured to save.
Bill clambered down the cliff, wet and completely flagged out,
The rescue team looked at Bill, he needed their support without any doubt.
The rescue operation was a complete success
The valiant efforts of Bill everyone did impress.

Bill was interviewed by the radio and local press,
The following question he was asked to address
"Do you feel proud to have saved two mens lives who were injured and ill?"
Bill smiled and slowly said, "It wasn't a bad effort for an old codger like me
who is over the hill."

Disagreements

All quarrels are usually destructive,
Certainly most are non productive.
Can turn into hate and bitterness,
Resulting in wars and all forms of stress.
A wise man will tell you whoever is in the wrong,
A smile and an apology is the best song.
It is the quickest way to heal any dispute,
The world would be a happier place if we all took that route.
If all disagreements could be talked calmly through,
It would save so much hassle, fretting and trouble too.
To turn your cheek can be very hard to do,
It takes a very strong heart to step back, smile and say, "After you."

Goodbye, My Love

Oh to be in England now spring is here,
Without you beside me my love, life is most drear.
The good lord took you into his fold last year,
My brightest star has vanished, that is most clear.
I'm alone without you and have lost my cheer,
The world moves on relentlessly it does appear.
Our two married sons have family to rear,
Their father's presence keeps your memory in our hearts most dear.
All your loved ones miss you most sincere,
You will not want your remembrance to mar our future happiness or interfere,
We honour and adore you for what you have brought us most dear.
Now we will stride firmly into the future without fear,
Seeking solace, love and compassion with you ever near.
Always remembering, who fortified our courage my dear,
You will never be forgotten precious wife and mother whom we revere.

After the Sunset...

After the sun goes down, the night in quickly does step,
The night enshrouds the now fading sunset.
Most of the world above water now goes to sleep,
But life never rests in the ocean deep.

On earth the predators of the night come into their own,
Throughout the land they fly and roam.
Under the cover of darkness they stalk and wait,
Their victims unaware with death they have an early date.

The owl glides with ghost like silence over field and tree,
Any movement spotted will end in catastrophe,
For mouse, for rat or rabbit or any other in the food chain,
Every night this hunt must go on again and again.

The mouse scurries across the forest floor
Its urgent need is insects or nuts for its food store.
Ant, spider or bug that mouse finds in its way,
Crunch, crunch, it wont see another day

At night fall bats take to the air in their multitude
Flying with mouths wide open, swallowing small fly in their plenitude
They clean the air and enjoy their midnight feast
It takes millions of flies to satisfy these little beasts.

Mother Nature is alive and active 24 hours a day it would seem
Whilst you and I are at home at night abed and dream.
The wildlife at night is fighting for its survival
When the sun sets, night will be seeking its revival.

The Good Abbot's Vanishing House

It was going to be a long, long night
We were lost on the moors, not a soul in sight.
I reckon we had walked over twenty miles that day
Now it was obvious we had lost our way.
According to our map the hostel we had booked was a few miles back
We certainly didn't pass one, because we were on the wrong track.
The night is falling fast and drizzle is setting in
Should we put up our tent and eat our dinner out of a tin.
We looked at each other to make a decision
How to continue this miserable part of our mission.

Jim said, "I vote we snug in while we have a little light.
Doing it later in the dark wont enhance our plight."
We tested the wind so we could pitch in a safe spot
On the west side of a hill seemed a good plot.
While Harry was sorting out our gear
I thought in the distance a hunting horn I could hear.
I climbed to the top of the hill to see
Whatever the sound of the noise could be.
At the top I espied a light that appeared not far away
I called Harry up to see and have his say.

We both agreed we should head for that welcoming sight
The wind was rising, the rain pouring, a very unpleasant night.
We packed up and walked on for about an hour
The weather was developing its unpleasant power.
We reached a small cottage, front door ajar
The oil lamp on the table shone like a star.
We entered in and shouted, "Anyone there?"
Of human life the cottage was bare.
We piled the fire with logs set aside
The flames roared high and its fierce heat was not to be denied.

On the dresser was a fresh loaf and cheese
A jug of ale and fruit, all set to please
The appetite of two hungry young men indeed
How come they were there to satisfy our need.
That night lightning flashed, the storm raged
In that cottage we were safe and content and soon sleep engaged.
Next morning the storm had abated
We finished last night's repast and wrote a note that stated
That the host's hospitality was gratefully appreciated.

We moved off and eventually came upon "The Welcome Inn"
That night in the bar we met the host who had a cheery grin.
He said, "Last night we had one of the worst storms ever
Sleeping out on the moor wouldn't have been very clever.
Did you find a cave or alternative shelter?
Being out in that storm you wouldn't have survived that belter."
We explained to him that we had stayed in a cottage
Thereby avoiding the driving wind, rain and the lightning voltage.
We couldn't understand how this shelter was warm and dry
Food available, no one was in, or why?

The host said, "Let me tell you a story
It's about an event that occurred in this moor's history.
It was said an abbot got lost in the wilds of our moor
A storm blew up, snow fell, more than he could endure.
He died. As good men do, he went to Heaven on high
He didn't want this way for any other men to die.
So he persuaded God that on any stormy night
When strangers are lost and in a desperate plight
To provide a haven, safe and warm
To protect them against Nature's ferocity and storm.

A hunting horn is blown to attract the travellers attention
Who blows it is always a point of contention.
The house is open, door ajar, inviting as you did see
Providing sustenance and shelter all entirely free.
The morning after when the visitors leave
This cottage vanishes—it is hard to believe.
Until the next dark and stormy night
And lost travellers are a sorry sight."

Harry said to Jim, "To a miracle we have been witness
Without that haven we would have been in severe distress.
We should thank him for his mercy and applaud
That we both enjoyed the privilege of sheltering in the arms of the Good Lord."

Skateboarding

Tweedle Dum and Tweedle Dee one day over tea
Decided to go on a skateboarding spree
They picked a country road which was traffic free
It was on a hill with a gentle slope
That was the part on which they could cope
When it got steeper they didn't have a hope.

On the steep slope they raced faster and faster
The skateboard spree had now become a disaster
In this situation they were not the master
At the bottom of the hill was Mr. Giles' farm
This very thought gave them both great alarm
If they crashed they could come to much harm.

Fortunately Farmer Giles' gate was open wide
They swept through it and into a dung heap they did slide
This pile of muck sure dented their pride
They got up bruised and battered and smelt very strong
They both agreed this venture had gone very wrong
And that with skateboards they did not belong.

Next day cleaned up and having tea
They were deciding what would be their next spree
Making sure their future choice would be disaster free.

The Flying Vee

Many things in Nature make you wonder and marvel
In their simplicity, their efficiency, their beauty you must revel.
I lift my head and look into the sky,
I espy a flock of geese flying high
In their distinctive vee formation the world knows,
It serves them well whichever way the wind blows.

It increases their flying range by seventy percent,
When a gaggle of geese is in the ascent.
When a goose flags in this aerial situation
Its fellow travellers honk it to relight its determination.
Every bird in this flying vee is important
Every bird is vital and must not relent.

This is wonderful as far as I can see
How it happened is a complete mystery to me.
How did all this come about?
This instinct is now inherent at birth no doubt.
How long did it take the geese to find out
The laws of nature to overcome and flout.

Many birds now have this great flying ability
Increasing their flying power and capability.
It allows them to follow the seasons over land and sea
It is wonderful, miraculous, beautiful, it's still a puzzlement to me!

I Dream

I dream, I dream, I dream,
When I hold your hand and we walk alone in the park,
When I caress you lovingly in the dark.
When I kiss you on the lips with tender care,
When you smile at me I feel contentment so rare.
When I am without you my heart misses a beat,
When I am without you I feel so deplete.
When we take our nuptial vows, when we are wed.
When we shall reach marital fruition in our wedding bed.
When we are honey mooning on the shores of the South Sea,
When we shall swim together, in harmony, just you and me.
I dream and dream and dream and wonder how
The world has been so kind to me
To secure the wondrous love of a woman such as thee.

The Candle

The Good Father met Mr. and Mrs. O'Conner in the street,
Gave a big smile and with his usual cheery greet,
Said, "How are you both, have you had any family yet?"
They responded sadly, "No, Father, no children have we been able to beget."

The Good Father smiled and said, "Next week I shall be going to Rome,
I shall light a candle asking the Good Lord for your family to no longer postpone.
Four years later the Good Father met Mrs. O'Conner , she looked tired,
Beamed, said, "Mrs. O'Conner, I hope you are well, any family have you yet sired?"
Mrs. O'Conner responded, "In four years we have had four sets of twins,
Mr. O'Conner has just gone to Rome to blow the candle out and ask the Lord to
    forgive us our sins."

An Autumn Highlight

It is a November afternoon, overcast and dank
We have come to walk along the Medway river bank.
The weather is mild, at least we have got that to thank.
In bad conditions this walk is high in our rank.

Most of the walk which is three miles long
Because it is covered by trees if it rains we can't go wrong.
The path is covered in leaves red, brown and gold
When on the trees they are a sight to behold.

Now on the ground they have become a mush
Soon, with more rain, they will become slush.
When we walk along the bank appreciating Winter is nearly here
Thinking of past sunshine days to bring us cheer.

Then we hear the honking of a gaggle of Canadian geese
Their strident noise breaks Nature's peace.
There were about sixty of them squabbling, causing furore
We couldn't see what had caused this uproar.

As we walked along the bank they swam beside us
Then suddenly all was quiet—gone was all the fuss.
They paced us until we got to the lock
Then they rose as one and flew off in a flock.

They ascended about a hundred feet into a grey sky,
They showed how strong and graceful they could fly.
They circled around twice, decided where to go,
As smooth as clockwork to their next destination they did flow

It was a grand sight to see
It made our day we both did agree
The rain that threatened all the day
During our walk blessed us, and kept away.

Sitting at home that night in front of our comforting fire
We mused over Natures beauty, her activity, all the world could only admire.

Welcome to Heaven

Three nuns were standing at the pearly gate
Of heaven waiting for God to decide their fate.
Each one would be given a test,
Of a Holy question—divinity at its best.

Each question must be answered right,
If wrong the loser could be in a desperate plight.
God asked the first nun "Can you answer this,
Who was the first man and woman on earth creating heavenly bliss."

Without a qualm she replied, "Adam and Eve"
"Well done, you are right, I do believe."
God asked the second nun "Where did Adam and Eve meet,
Can you name the town or the street?"

The second nun was not going to be caught,
She replied, "In the garden of Eden," without any thought.
God nodded, with a smile, turned to the Mother Superior,
"Your question will be harder to show you are not inferior.

What did Eve say to Adam when they first met?"
Mother Superior was anxious, this answer was difficult to get.
"Dear God," she spluttered out. "That's a very hard one."
"Well done," said God. "Welcome to Heaven and join in the fun."

A Great Blue Sky

It is early summer, our England nestles under a great blue sky,
A few billowing clouds meander gently by.
A pleasant breeze is wafting off the sea,
The sun beams down making it a wonderful day for you and me.

Our countryside is lush and green,
Every where thrusting nature is to be seen.
Our feathered friends busily feed their hungry brood,
The chicks always impatient to get their food.

The fallow deer, the lowing cattle chew the vibrant pasture,
They feed in total comfort and leisure.
The vixen is guarding her cubs around her den,
The fox is hunting hoping to catch a big juicy hen.

The colourful Kingfisher is perching beside the river bank waiting
For the fish to rise, its future ended, there is no debating.
The farmers fields, ploughed, sowed, now filled with their designated crop
To many it would be a disaster if we didn't produce a pleasure giving hop.

With good winter rains the rivers, streams and reservoirs are filled to the brim,
Enabling our fish stocks to thrive and swim.
We rest, play, picnic, love, in the shade of a great oak tree
We relax and let our thoughts and dreams roam free.

Mother Nature in her benevolence makes it a great world in which to stay,
That it will continue we sincerely hope and pray.
To our Eternal Father who sits on his throne most high,
It would be wonderful if we could live forever under a great blue sky.

Spring Green

To my father a most wonderful colour was spring green,
When it arrived he declared this winter was now a has-been.
When spring green quietly appeared and peeked out
On the buds of trees, shrubs and grass that was about.

We knew it was too early to shed our heavy winter overcoat,
Jack Frost was still close by to freeze and poke.
Mother Nature has always been the greatest power on earth,
Controlling life from death to birth.

As winter melts away, temperatures rise, spring green grows stronger,
New life on earth by winter is contained no longer.
The Floribunda thrust up through the good earth and has its day,
Snowdrops and crocuses will have had their annual display.

Daffodils and gladioli bloom forth in their golden delight,
Dear Mother Nature after the dark winter spring is a most welcome sight.
We know winter is necessary to allow the earth to rest,
It eliminates the weakest, only the strongest survive its hazardous test.

When spring green arrives in England we all revive,
Seasonal breezes and sunshine makes us all want to be alive.
We look forward to summer with expectation and gladness,
Compensating us for winter's season of wind rain and dampness.
Spring green should bring a smile to everyone's face,
Its arrival always makes the world a far happier place.

The Village Fete at Abbey Dove

My family and I live in the village of Abbey Dove
We have a High Street, a pond, a village green, what is more,
We are only a mile away from the seashore.
A century ago many of our houses were at the sea's edge, that's folklore.
We still endure in winter the strong prevailing ocean wind,
For days on end its force it does not rescind.
Many of our trees and shrubs have learnt to survive
By learning to lean and grow before Mother Nature's force in order to stay alive.

Our winters may be hard, but we have great summers too,
The farmers know how to manage the land, and work the seasons through.
The last ten years they have enjoyed a financial heyday,
The crops have been very good, and its golden egg did lay.
Mum and Dad had two children, Maggie my elder sister, and Tony that's me.
We were all born in Abbey Dove, which was the world as far as we could see.
The high lights of the year were harvesting, Christmas and our annual fete day.
The day of the fete was always held in mid September, come what may.

It was always held in Farmer Jobbins' field, next to our village green,
Betwixt the two stood our large village oak tree, ancient, tall, proud and did not lean,
It had withstood the storms and gales that Mother Nature in her fury at it threw
In our country such healthy and magnificent giants were few.
I know I am only fourteen, but I can never recall it ever rained on our fete day,
Everyone comes to enjoy themselves, come early, determined to stay.
Of course there were stalls galore, the vendors came from miles around,
To village folk like us their fancy goods, new tools and new ideas would astound.

All ladies love clothes, many stalls displayed them with that in mind,
These choices were only here once a year, so, dear lord, be kind.
Let our ladies joyfully search and buy their unexpected find,
To miss this opportunity would be such an awful bind.
When the fetes visitors entered Farmer Jobbins' field,
Everyone over eighteen was given a ticket which would yield
A glass of apple cider served in the marquee,
Drawn from six casks donated by good Farmer Jobbins given free.

Dad saw a raincoat which he was in urgent need of,
Tried it on, it was ideal, fitted like a glove.
Mum being the shrewd one, said it wasn't good enough and too dear,
The vendor dropped his price and still Mum would not hear,
She started to walk away, the vendor said without hesitation
He saw he was going to lose this sale, he had to save the situation,
"Buy this coat and I will give you a brolly and a bonnet too"
Mum turned, nodded her agreement, closed the deal, would not you?
Maggie chose the bonnet and put it on straight away,
It was white, embroidered with pretty flowers, it made her day.
When she strolled around the fete in her new headgear
She received many compliments from the young men, which to her were very dear.
The young ones loved the roundabout turned by hand
Riding up and down on the wooden horses was simply grand.
It didn't matter who was going to win this race,
Especially as all the riders and horses were travelling at the same pace.

Dad spotted something he knew I greatly desired
When he showed me, my passion was fired.
There stood at the end of the second stall
A Jack Hobbs cricket bat and cricket ball.
The bat was a little big for me now I know
But in a year's time that would not be so.
It would be cleaned and oiled and put away
Ready for next May when cricket we would again play.

Mum had it in mind as the children would soon be grown up,
It would be lovely to get a pup.
The local kennels had their show next to the village green,
Where thirty-four puppies of many breeds could be touched, cuddled and seen.
We got to the pitch where the pups were barking excitedly at their best,
You could spot the healthy ones, they were jumping about with zest.
Their brown eyes, wagging tails, happy yapping would put most folks hearts to the test.
Their message, "Please take me home and I will be a wonderful guest"
Mum took over thirty minutes to make her choice,
We all agreed with her decision with one voice.
He was a black and white cocker spaniel to be called Ben,
Dad would collect him from the kennels tomorrow around ten.

The china smashing stall is always a great hit!
Ten balls a penny, throw them and break every bit
Of the old crockery, sitting there waiting to be bashed.
Young men line up to show their skills at having their targets smashed.
This amusement is very popular and profitable indeed,
Anyone wishing to raise money for charity should heed.
The proceeds gained here go to the church's local orphanage,
With thirty children to look after, to support and encourage.

Through out the afternoon there are three periods of entertainment,
Taking place in the middle of Farmer Jobbins' field, a suitable arrangement.
First to perform are the Morris Dancers, lively and full of spirit,
Encouraging all to join and dance with them, to everyone's delight.
An hour of this hectic activity calls for a rest,
A falconer has arrived to show his birds at their best.
He has a group of eight all very well trained,
The audience sat, watched, absorbed as the birds actions were explained.

These monarchs of the air dived, raced, chased, spun and flew at great speed,
The prey with the falcons skills had no chance to escape, we all agreed.
Another hour had passed enjoyed by an enthralled crowd,
When the exhibition was over they clapped long and loud.
The last entertainment was a choir from our local school,
There numbers had been increased with local elders, whose talents they did pool,
The songs they sang we all knew and enjoyed,
We were all invited to sing together, our vocal cords were fully employed.

The church clock chimed out it was six o'clock,
It was telling us all it was time to take stock.
We had met friends old and new on this festive day,
Now we would be homeward bound, each going their every way.
When we got home our family were in a tired and happy state,
So much to talk about, to compare, to relate.
We sat down to supper hardly noticing what was on our plate,
To all of us it had been a wonderful day and another very successful fete.

I Miss You

My true love passed away at the age of three score and ten,
We had been married for forty-five years when
She died suddenly of a tremendous stroke,
My life was shattered, my heart was broke.
I miss you, I miss you, I miss you.

Pamela and I had been blessed with three sons, one two and three,
They had all married, had children to continue the family tree.
They were wonderful in supporting in my time of sorrow,
Without them I couldn't have faced the uncertainty of tomorrow.
I miss you, I miss you, I miss you.

My father taught me "Cry and you cry alone" that is very true,
Without you I didn't know what to do.
I was father and granddad to my sons' families,
My only purpose left was to help them fulfil their future strategies.
I miss you, I miss you, I miss you.

Yes, I got great satisfaction in undertaking this task,
But missing you, those feelings I cannot mask.
I press on, getting slower every day,
Smiling at life, helping out when I can and may.
I miss you, I miss you, I miss you.

To my loved ones, I tell them I am pleased to go.
My time has come, I just want them to know,
I thank them all with my love for helping me along,
But it is only to you that my heart does belong.
I want to be with you in the great sky above.
Holding hands, embracing you, kissing you with all my love.
I miss you, I miss you, I miss you.

My Inauguration to Love

It was in 1951 in August when I was nearly nineteen,
On reflection, a long time ago it would seem.
Because of my ability to play a strong game of chess,
I was invited to play in the British Chess Championship, the under 21s no less.

I accepted the invitation. All expenses paid.
To play other up and coming young folk in my grade.
It was to be played in the central hall of Nottingham University,
An ideal setting to play this historic game in this learned faculty.

On the Saturday before this forthcoming event,
A return ticket to catch the coach to Nottingham was sent.
I boarded the coach at 9 o'clock for my journey to begin,
I was going to Nottingham, to display my chess prowess and win!

Five hours later I arrived at the city of Robin Hood fame,
I followed instructions to find my allocated accommodation, for me my bed to claim.
It was situated in a terraced row of houses, if I remember right,
The house was small, looked tired, not a reassuring sight.

I knocked on the door with a little trepidation,
My first reaction was rather down on my expectation.
The door was opened by a lady with a lovely smile,
"Welcome, young man," she said in a manner which would anyone beguile.

"Your three other friends have already arrived,
They are having some tea and homemade cake," she said with pride.
"Come in and join us, we will help you to settle in,
I know tomorrow your chess tournament will begin."

Mrs. Noakes was our hostess for the following week,
No fault in her hospitality of which we could speak.
During the University terms she catered for 4 students.
Provided bed, breakfast and evening meal with propriety and prudence.

The bedrooms were basic, each shared by two,
2 beds, a wardrobe, a table and 2 chairs did do.
Her cooking was great, plentiful, and tasty too,
She wasn't obtrusive, and left you free to do what you wanted to.

The evening meal was at seven, she did not like you being late,
Her meals were freshly cooked, and first rate
She liked the dinner to be over by eight,
She liked to be in bed by nine, that was her nightly date.

Sunday morning the competitors met in the conference hall,
To start their ten game tournaments, the winners win, the losers fall.
The beauty of chess, you cannot blame ones result on lady luck,
The best man on the day wins, the loser gets the duck.

After the first days play, the hall was closed, and everyone retired,
Mrs Noakes four guests sat down to dinner, now hungrily desired.
When dinner was finished, our hostess offered her guests the following information,
Whether they valued it was at their own instigation.

"In the town of Nottingham the ladies outnumber the men by ten to one.
If you ask me why, I will tell you how this is come.
Players the cigarette manufacturers employs 30,000 women or more,
And only 2000 men, now you see the score.

When the ladies know there are new men in town,
Some ladies without doubt will track them down.
Don't be surprised if we get a knock on the door,
A pretty face will invite you to a drink, or on to a dance floor."

Us young men smirked, we had never encountered anything like that before,
We were taken aback when thirty minutes later there was a tap on the front door.
Standing there were four beautiful nurses, early twenties, all in uniform,
Marion the leader said with a smile sincerely, subtly shy, a little forlorn.

"We are looking for partners to help us while the night away,
Wondered if you would like to join us during your short stay.
We usually go for a drink, play skittles, or go to a dance,
We will bring you back safely, of getting lost there is no chance."

Well three of us took up this tempting invitation,
What else could three healthy men do in this alluring situation
A short walk just around the corner, was the local inn,
Well supported, but on the ground numbers of men were thin.

Marion, the Robin Hood damsel, who else could it be?
Anyway, she latched on to me, she was wonderful company.
In spite of my shyness, her caresses warmed me to her beauty,
Sooner or later this man was going to do his duty!

We moved from the inn to the local dance hall,
We danced all evening until the " The Last Waltz " was the call.
She smiled sweetly. "Come and have coffee in my flat."
It would have been rude not to accept an offer like that!

It seemed only minutes later, and we were sitting on her bed
"We can have coffee now, or you can make love to me instead.
I have to be on duty in my hospital ward in case you don't know,
In forty minutes time I will have to go.

I must admit my passion and heart was all aglow,
You could say I lost my virginity in my emblazoned show.
When the fire was spent Marion quietly said to me,
"Can we see each other tomorrow night" was her gentle plea.

Tomorrow night, I am not on duty, I shall be totally free.
We can go out for a meal, play some skittles, and then come back with me.
I accepted this invitation without hesitation and joy,
I was not going to miss out on the pleasures between girl and boy.

Next day in the chess tournament, I did not concentrate,
I drew one game, lost the second deservedly to a weaker player, that was my fate.
I was thinking and relishing the thought of my evening date,
I told Mrs Noakes no dinner tonight thank you, I will be back late.

Mrs Noakes did not bat an eyelid, I think she understood,
She smiled knowingly. "Hope it all turns out for your happiness and good."
I met Marion on her doorstep at the time agreed,
We walked arm in arm to a small restaurant, which complemented our need.

Over our meal, we talked, got to know each other much better,
Realising I was going home on Saturday, I mentioned we should keep in touch by letter.
The dinner service was painfully slow, the meal took far longer than expected,
She suggested we skipped skittles, and go immediately to her flat was the option selected.

We spent the evening enjoying the company of each other,
Responding to satisfy the needs as would an unsatisfied lover.
It was early morning when we agreed I had to go,
All good things come to an end, I know my disappointment did show.

Marion said, "Next Friday night is the only time we can meet,
Our mutual enjoyment till then we must forfeit.
I am honour bound to meet my nursing obligations,"
To both of us this was an understandable frustration.

The next two days I decided to play the best chess I could,
To my sponsors I knew they wanted me to prove I was good.
Harkening back, I suppose I played well in the tournament through out,
But at the back of my mind there was a shadow of doubt.

Would Marion be there when Friday came?
Without her, life would never be the same.
When I returned on Thursday evening to Mrs Noakes abode,
A package had arrived for me, which all my fears did erode.

A small package awaited me, much to my surprise,
As I read the message with it my spirits did surely rise.
"Dear Robert, see you tomorrow. Love M."
The present was a delightful writing pen.

Next day at the chessboard I played at my best,
My new love had given me confidence and zest.
I won my last two games, I played really well,
I came second in the tournament, which was great as far as I could tell.

That evening Marion and I dined on a boat on the River Trent,
We wandered along the river banks, amid the osiers heaven sent.
We were spellbound in each others company,
We loved the night away, dreaming only of her and me.

Next morning we parted, she said she was moving, that she would write,
I felt ten feet tall, the future could only be bright.
I had done well at chess, my new found love was a total delight,
I would love her forever, with all my might.

A week later a letter came through the front door,
It was from Marion to tell me the score.
She had gone to Switzerland for an operation on the brain,
If she did not have it soon, her life would soon drain.

She thanked and blessed me for our short romance,
What life she had left, our relationship it would enhance.
She gave no address, but said she would write again,
I tried desperately to find her, but it was in vain.

A month later her parents passed a letter written just before,
Death was taking her through his door.
Again no address, Marion wished to leave a clean slate,
No ties, no regrets, just a memory of our love and happiness to relate.

Her passing came as a shock you understand,
My once euphoric future now lay waste and unplanned.
This joy and tragedy came so quickly joined together,
I am sure I will remember them forever and ever.

Six months later at our chess club's Annual General Meeting,
The chairman welcomed us all with his usual cheerful greeting.
Congratulated me on my successful inauguration to chess at the Nottingham University,
Not knowing of my other inauguration to love and adversity.

A Summer's Day

I love to take a book and sit under my ancient oak tree.
It stands beside a small stream that runs free.
I enjoy its cool shade on a hot summers day,
Meditate and let my thoughts peacefully stray.

I listen to the silence, or natures country sounds,
Here the bustle of ones presence is out of bounds.
Hush! I hear the streams waters quietly wend their merry way,
Flowing over stones and rocks that permanently stay.

Catch the drone of the busy bumble bee,
Collecting the pollen from the flowers in this pleasant lea.
In the distance I hear the bleat of grazing sheep,
Their gentleness allows you to count them in your sleep.

Settled in this oak, is a squirrels family of four,
If you stay quiet and still long enough they will come scratching at your door.
Only twice I have seen a kingfisher visit our stream,
In summer time it is too shallow to catch fish in, it would seem.

The birds which nest in the branches above,
Chirp and sing to complete the memory I love.
I hear with dismay the creak of the wooden gate opening nearby,
My friend has come to collect me, and I must say goodbye.
Return to my normal life, and come what may,
Always longing to revisit my stream on another Summer's Day.

My First Dance

Nearly fifty years ago, yes that's how long it was
Fifty years ago I went to my first dance because
Young men and ladies would meet in hope at this romantic scene
To dance the night away with a partner of their dream.

My dad advised me to take lessons at a dancing school,
So on the dance floor I would look competent, not a fool.
It was a young mans duty to impress upon the lady of his choice,
Of his desirability, his capability, supported with an authoritative voice.

I took lessons on how to dance the waltz, the tango, the quick step and the foxtrot too,
So when the appropriate music was played I would not be in a stew.
Dad lent me a suit, one he rarely had the opportunity to wear,
Made me promise I would treat it with the greatest of care.

My best friend and I planned to go to the next town hall dance,
As we saw it we had a great chance
Of capturing the hearts of two lovely girls,
Exhibiting our manliness, our joie de vivre, our dancing and twirls.

The big night arrived, we thought we would turn up thirty minutes late,
Playing hard to get, we hoped to get the girls in a state.
When we got there the cupboard was bare,
All the young folk had chosen their dancing partners to make their pair.

Most dances tended to have a surplus of the opposite sex,
We never found out why it was not written into this text.
We learnt our lesson, and at the next town hall dance,
We were there at the opening of the doors ready to prance.

We both found partners and were soon ready for the off,
The music played and I felt happy as a toff
We soon learnt that the ladies had a choice too,
They changed their partners often, to determine with whom they wished to woo.

It was many months later I met Janet my wife,
We became friends, started courting, then she became my wife.
Fifty years later we still glide, a little more slowly around the dance floor
Enjoying our dancing, enjoying our life, loving each other, who could ask for
anything more.

He Was Well-to-Do

He was not rich but he was well-to-do
Retired early in life because he was well-to-do.
Had a manservant and cook because he was well-to-do
Had his own horse and carriage as he was well-to-do.

Dressed smart and in fashion as he was well-to-do.
He received invitations galore as he was well-to-do.
He lived in a large fine house as he was well-to-do.
Leased it on a low rent as he was well-to-do.

All folk must die even if they be well-to-do,
He had planned for this occasion being well-to-do.
They buried him with dignity and respect as he was well-to-do
He entered heaven on the premise of being a well-to-do.

Jesus asked him what exactly is a well-to-do?
Rather astonished he thought his answer through.
He replied "One who is neither rich nor poor,
One who has his own independence and front door,

One who plays his part in society,
Does not depend on another for charity,
Gives advice to those in need with clarity,
Treating all with liberalism and parity"

Jesus smiled and gently spoke in a firm tone
"All your life you have been well-to-do and alone,
Neither giving or receiving love which I cannot condone,
As heaven is full of love you must find another home."

The Future Is Yours

The lonely figure walking through the yew tree glade
Visiting the sombre gravestone recently engraved.
Her thoughts and memories lingering in the past
How life with her departed partner went by so fast.

And now alone time seems to stand so still
The reason for living seems pointless, dull and chill.
We visit this earth only on one occasion
Each with our own soul, each with our own persuasion.

It is but a brief stay in relation to time
Some would say life is without reason or rhyme.
Most of us, God willing, have a choice
To live, to love, enjoy this earth and have a voice.

Therefore my love, do not waste a moment in sad contemplation
Life goes on, of that you need no explanation.
Your past love will make you surely aware
His spirit has gone to a place of love and care.

He wants your remaining stay on earth not to be filled with remorse
But for you to enjoy with others the future of course.
Your happiness or sadness as the case may be
Will spread to your closest and your family.

Cry and you cry alone—a saying so true
Smile and the world smiles with you.
Think positively of happiness and the good you can do
And on your gravestone will be etched
"Thank you for the happiness you have given us
God Bless You."

The Tree on Our Village Green

There is a grand old oak tree on our village green,
It is said, it has been there forever to many it does seem.
In the county library, it was recorded over two hundred years ago,
The thickness of its trunk and branches indicates this could be so.

This ancient oak does dominate our village green.
In all seasons its splendour adds strength to our country scene.
It has survived gales, storms, tempests and the foulest of weather,
Its great might and solidness is what holds it together.

When winter comes, it gently subsides into its winters sleep,
Also do the families of squirrels who live in this trunk, most deep.
They have already stored the fruits of their generous benefactor,
Its acorns to nourish them through the bleak times ahead, a chilling factor.

Some birds that nest in the comfort of this great oak tree,
When winter approaches, to warmer climates they do flee.
Those who stay appreciate the protection this giant has in its ambit,
They will stay until spring opens its reviving gambit.

When spring comes, its birds and foliage start to proclaim its seasonal glory,
The birds sing, the squirrels in the branches frolic, winter is now history.
The villagers look and see that spring has come to stay,
When their oldest inhabitant doth its cloak of light green display.

In the summer its foliage provides shade against the fierce sun,
Many, many families have picnicked here in the cool, having fun,
In the evening in the cool of the night, it becomes a lover's meet,
Here one can show ones affections and be totally discreet.

Our friendly oak has witnessed many a cricket match,
The club's spectators enjoying its cover from the sun or rainy patch.
It offers the same cover when a football game is on,
Or when the village fete is held, the oak plays its part, all said and done.

When Autumn creeps in, in hand with the waning sun and darkening sky,
Our proud oak sheds its leaves, yields its fruit, for nature it cannot defy.
The squirrels, moles, mice and many more,
Will secrete this oaks produce into their own winter store.

When Winter comes the oak will be at peace with all the land
It will survive the season of cold, wet, and snow as nature planned.
It will look forward to the harkening of Spring as we all do
When the tattoo of life rises up again, to begin its cycle of the earth to renew.

Another Year

January is the month that ushers in the New Year
Hoping Winter is gently moving to our rear.

February will shower us with rain, snow and sleet
Chill winds make one rub hands and stamp feet.

March pulls in high winds and romping breezes
We still get caught out with sudden freezes.

With April comes the scent of Spring
And birds with anticipation delightedly sing.

May heralds in the new born of many a breed
Creating more and more mouths to feed.

June at last, the sun beams on us all around
Flowers bloom, bees are busy, Nature's glory does abound.

July's forecast is sunshine with intermittent showers
The days stretch with long and pleasant hours.

August arrives and produces the fruits of the season
From tiny seeds, they grow without rhyme or reason.

September sees Summer sadly and slowly in decline
The year is mellowing, like a good wine.

October with its colour brings in Autumn
Season of mists and maturing sun.

November comes in dull and wet, Winter has arrived
With its chill winds you wonder how the World has survived.

December enters remembered for its Christmas cheer
You hug the blazing fire and wonder why we are here.

Another year has drawn to its inevitable end
And Nature's cycle turns again on which our World will depend.

A Friend

A man is fortunate and wealthy indeed
If he has a friend when he is in need.
When the going is good, when times are bad
When happiness abounds, when occasions are sad.

When the sun shines, when furious tempests blow
When prospects are bright, when troubles flow
In all times, wet or dry, whatever the end
Beside you will always be a true friend.

Look around, contemplate with hand on heart
Can you tell fair weather friends or true friends apart?
Which is which, in ascertaining, where do you start?
The test of time, a strong occasion will produce the right heart.

A true friend is created through trust, love, respect and care
Can you respond with more if you dare.
You and your friend will have a bond to treasure
Each other's company will generate pleasure.

When you have a loved one or friend so true
In most people's lives they are too few.
A friend is life's precious gift to you
Respect, love and care for them and they will return it to you know who.

The Intruders

At the dead of night the new moon shines supreme
On the woods at the edge of the village green.
The tawny owl sits motionless listening to hear his prey
So that he can feed his brood before the oncoming day.

This predator glides as silent as a ghost of the night
Preferring to finish his business ere to the morning light.
Hush, a ground leaf, twig or grass is shaken
Whoosh, another mouse, or titbit by the owl is taken.

Hark, there is another movement on the ground
Stealthy treading feet create a quiet menacing sound.
Moving towards the house of the squire
Burglars determine to steal what they desire.

The night is shattered with the sound of broken glass
The intruders plan has come to pass
Then two gunshots ring out loud and clear
This night will cost the burglars dear.

The squire it seems was ready for their attack
This doughty and elderly gentleman courage did not lack.
Those wounded criminals will tomorrow be in jail
And soon after that the gallows will prevail.

The dark countryside and wood returns to quietness and serenity
After the disturbance caused by greedy humanity.
The owl sits patiently listening, listening, listening
The moon through the clouds is glistening, glistening, glistening.

Hush, Mother Nature is in full control again
The owl plays his lead part in the food chain.
The mouse, the shrew, the vole and kin
In turn are predators on the others without sin.

A Smile

A smile is what the world loves to see
It creates a warm bond from you to me.
A smile opens doors and one's heart
It reduces anguish when one has to part.

A smile is encouragement one always needs
A reward and thank you for good deeds.
A smile is a lovely opening gambit
Welcoming you into ones personal ambit.

A smile can dispel one's gloom
Bring back joy and banish doom.
A smile will come when you are well and happy
Help to cheer those sad and snappy.

A smile brings back the verve to be alive
Tells misery to be gone and take a dive.
A smile can be a thank you—an expression
It can send a most positive indication.

A smile can flow from everyone on earth
Its in us from maturity and our birth.
It would be wonderful if we all smiled many times a day
Making living for all of us one long and happy holiday.

My Valentine

I met you through a friend on a blind date,
I knew then I wanted you as my soul mate.
Peter took me to a dance to meet his girl friend and you,
He introduced us, and we danced the night through.

When I went home I was walking on air,
You had promised me another date, I felt we were making a pair.
I took you on my motor bike down to the coast,
To show you off to my friends and boast.

Of the beautiful and gorgeous girl who had captured my heart,
As the song says, "From whom I will never wish to part."
Julie my love I have never felt like this before,
You will always be the girl I will truly adore.

Now you have accepted my hand in marriage,
I'm already driving the horse and carriage
To the local church where we are to be wed,
In the town where we were both born and bred.
The day we are married you will become a treasure of mine,
You will forever be my most precious Valentine.

The Boot Fair

It is a bit of fun, you will pick up a bargain or two,
The stalls offer you a selection of something old, something new.
I am told the origin of the boot fair
Was for families to sell their discarded ware.
Interested parties would meet on the field, car park or open ground
From car boots, the variety of chattels sold would you astound.
Entrepreneurs saw this an opportunity to grab and seize
With little overheads, this business venture would be a breeze.
Find an open space available at the weekend
Easily accessible for the stall holder and public to attend.
Ample car parking is a necessity of this scene
With good planning you have a very viable business scheme.

Today families, single mums and young bucks too
Display their goods, some well laid out, some without a clue.
Then there are those who are serious who wish to make a living
The local butcher shouting out the bargains he is giving.
Gardeners with flower trays with a great choice of vibrant shrub
The hamburger van and man enticing you with his tasty grub.
Folk selling tools, garden, plastic and clothing ware
So much for a pound each, refuse it you do not dare.
Back to the housewife disposing of her unwanted bric-a-brac
Including toys, books, videos, puzzles and out of date wall plaque.
She finds she enjoys the atmosphere of the fair
So she advertises to clear houses, also buys new from wholesalers' ware.

You must be keen to rise early at six or before
To ensure you get a prime site, so you will sell more.
Even the fairground is often very well represented
With various roundabouts, bouncy castles and swings all presented.
What you save on your bargains bought this way
You will spend on the kids and make their day.
Even charities put their foot through this door
Selling their donated goods which they could not sell before.
The public amble from stall to stall, stand and stare,
At the vendors selling goods both banal and bizarre.
Mementoes whose owners interest faded long ago
Seeking a new home, setting their buyers hearts aglow.

A good boot fair will be organised from the start
To attract paying stall holders to be part of their mart.
Enticing the customers to come along and buy
To search for bargains, admire the clothes, put them on and try.
When all is over the clearing up must be done
A part of the job which isn't always fun.
At the end of the day the site must be left tidy and secure
So to the next boot fair both stall holders and customers it will allure.

The Perfect Spot

It was a warm moonlit night,
It was summer, not a cloud in sight.
My true love and I were rambling around the park,
The quietness broken by an occasional dog bark.

We moved slowly, arms entwined down to the lake,
We knew the path we would take.
There was a tryst we knew well,
Where our love making would be secluded and gel.

My true love had brought a blanket with us,
He laid it on the grass without any fuss.
For the next few hours we would enjoy an idyllic dream,
Covered by the night and bathing in the moons beam.

Yes we were passionate, I can say nothing more,
Our love for each other exploded from every pore.
Now we are married and we walk in the park,
We are reminded of our love making in the dark.
Now our children picnic on that spot,
Not knowing in our younger days that was our heavenly spot.

Our Garden Visitors

Most of our visitors are the local birds who come in
Have to see what we have thrown out from our bread bin.
Mind you, it's the four sliced loaves we get each week from the local store,
Which broken up, encourage them to come back for more and. more.

Our garden has a spacious lawn, with many protective trees,
The birds fly in with safety, just as they please.
They come in sedate pairs, or descend in a flock,
Or we see the forceful character of a lone robin cock.

We have two statues with bird baths on their heads,
Where the birds bathe and drink, after they have been fed
Collared doves, thrushes, and lots of sparrows too
Frequent daily the birdhouse for seed and grain without ado.

Perhaps once a week, the gulls visit from our local seashore,
Any bread loose or cake on the lawn is their draw.
They pass over in a flock, if interested, they hover and hover,
Then dive down, snatch up the morsels without any bother.

Our smallest visitors are the variety of tits,
Who cling and peck at the hanging baskets of nuts, and other bits.
Always extremely nervous, they do not stay for long
A few quick pecks, they depart to pastures anew to sing their song..

Our family welcomes our many visitors of flight,
We give them sustenance, they give us the pleasure of their company and delight
Its great when the chicks are able to leave the nest,
And fly to our garden, to eat, and their wings to test.

Whatever the weather, come hail, sun or snow
Calm, storms, tempest, rain or just blow,
We love entertaining our feathered friends,
Pray our small gesture to Mother Nature is making some amends.
As Humanity is taking over the world to feed its voracious need,
To ignore the wonders of Mother Nature is folly indeed.

Our Garden Shed

In our garden we have a shed at the bottom end,
It's a comfortable size, roughly ten feet by ten.
It must be thirty years old or more,
Built by hand, with a solid concrete floor.

A few years ago electric points were added,
And the interior of the walls were padded,
With hardboard, to keep the heat in, and the cold out,
To make it comfortable, that's what it's all about.

The shed houses all the garden gear,
Side by side, with my table and office chair.
This sad looking shack has become my beloved den.
I visit often when I need solitude to pen.

I will not have a phone or fax put in,
To me its intrusion would be a sin
I must admit that humble shed of mine,
Gives me peace, serenity, which is quite divine.

Now my grandson knows where to find me,
When I'm missing from the house, and he is free,
He brings down his drawings, we share a mug of tea,
He shares his problems, the solutions we don't always agree.

One day, not far off, we shall move away,
To a smaller house, which at our age, should be our last permanent stay.
I only hope in the next garden that there is room,
To put in my shed, recreate my old den, and house the garden broom.

Our Lilac Tree in May

At the end of the garden stands a Lilac tree
In full blossom, a glorious sight to see.
Lovely, adorned in white petals, clothed in spring green, it augers well,
Its delicate fragrance and odour is a joy to smell.

The Lilac tree was planted in the year of my being,
We respect each others existence with mutual feeling.
As a young man, I was free to roam,
Knowing my Lilac tree would be abiding at home.

When I had a family with children three
They loved the garden, the pools, and the Lilac tree.
In the summer they play under the deciduous shade,
The sun twinkling through the leaves like a gentle cascade.

Now at the eventide of life I stand and stare,
Thank the Good Lord for what I have to enjoy and share.
I bless my wife, family and friends for comforting my life on earth
Also remembering that Lilac tree, a joy to me since my birth.

My Fair Lady

My Fair Lady shines brilliantly in the dark night sky,
When the clouds have disappeared she is alone, elegant, proud and high.
The stars twinkle and glisten to provide a royal backcloth,
Midnight lovers their allegiance to her do betroth.
The Moon is the Queen of Darkness to whom all she does behold.
She was present when our earth began we are told,
Our Lady watched over its conception, and how it would unfold.
This planet needs the radiance of both the sun and moon,
Without them our wonderful Earth would be dead in its womb.

Our Wonderful Trees

Where would we be without the blessing of a tree?
Their benefits are tremendous to everyone its plain to see.
Through its leaves it cleans the air we breathe,
The more trees we have, the less we heave.

The trees on this earth have served humanity well,
Their beauty, their foliage, their changing colours cast an enchanting spell.
So many birds depend on the trees to provide nest and food,
So many animals depend on trees, in order to bring up their brood.

Where trees grow, their roots bind the crumbling earth,
Without trees arid heath lands and deserts are given birth.
Trees are noted for attracting the rain,
Keeping the earth cool and moist, another gain.

Since the world began and Mankind needed fire,
Without kindling wood in the winter, mans future would be dire.
Early man used the leaves and the branches to make a thatch
Nomadic tribes could quickly build simple huts from scratch.

As the world's civilisation of man gradually matured,
It quickly appreciated the strength of wood, it became inured.
Wood was needed to build ships of great strength
To explore the world' s oceans, their breadth and length

Thinkers of the world realise the tremendous importance and beauty of wood
All life on this planet, know trees are vital to our existence for good.
When we walk down an avenue of trees
Stroll through a forest, admire the maturity, the beauty, as you please
Appreciate the Majesty, the diversity the durability of our wonderful trees.

When you look over our country's green and pleasant land
You admire the fields, the valleys, the rivers, the mountains, supported by trees
    most grand
The fruits of the trees bring pleasure and nourishment to our table
Is there any other natural product on earth which is so important and capable?

The World Goes Past My Window

I sit in my window at home in the bay
From there I can watch the world night and day.
I watch the traffic pass with fascination
Guessing their loads and their various destination.
Moving right, it could to the capital go
Moving left, it could to the ports flow.
The London Road of Rainham is busy indeed
Transporting cargo and folk according to need.

It is centuries ago when the Romans travelled this way
And built the highway, where it stands today.
I sit and dream of the generations and races
Who put their mode of travelling through its paces.
By foot, by horse, by cart and carriage
Today it's the motor that controls this passage.
It would seem as a Nation's needs grow
So will the London Road increase its traffic flow.

I wonder what the Roman invader would think
Seeing today how big now is his original link.
This thoroughfare is vital to all
Allowing public services to travel at call.
Our children travelling to school each day
Do not realise they are on the Old Roman Way.
Tonight I will lie down to sleep and dream
Of the sites and sounds this famous Way has seen.

He Came, He Saw, She Conquered

I admit I am an old thirty-three
I still sit on the tree of virginity.
When I finish my office work and go home
I do hate my empty cold flat and being alone.
I work hard to keep my figure slim and in good shape
Hoping Mr. Right will admire and gape.
Hoping he will boldly ask me for a date
They say it is too early to be resigned to a spinster's fate.

I have already tried and played the dating game,
But the propositions I received put me to shame.
They say a girl in my position should take a chance,
But, I wouldn't give any of my proposers a second glance.
They say you are more successful to hunt in pairs
Jenny joins me, my friend from the flat upstairs.
At weekends we go to the local dance
To see what beaus we can entrance.

Jenny and I know we must smile and listen,
Always put out a welcome sign and glisten.
A few years ago we dreamed of lovers above our station
Now a smile from most men brings us elation.
We were becoming despondent that was true,
We both needed love and companionship, now long overdue.
One Summer's evening after work we were walking round the park
Nightfall was closing in, it was beginning to get dark.

We heard from the bushes a cry for help and a groan
We went there and found an elderly man, badly beaten and alone.
Quickly I called an ambulance on my mobile phone
We carried him on to the lawn to help his pain atone.
We wrapped his head to stem the flow
Of blood caused by a very heavy blow.
Fifteen minutes later the ambulance arrived on the scene
Whisked all three of us back to the hospital to the waiting team.

The old gentleman was sedated, had a lot of stitches put in
We girls cleaned up, then explained to the police what we knew of this sin.
We made our way home, content that we had done our good deed
We had a glass of wine, then sleep was our only need.
Five days later there was a knock on my front door
There stood our gentleman, head bandaged, still very sore.
Beside him, his son who had come to assist
He gave me a smile that I couldn't resist.

He said, "We have come to thank you for the help you gave Dad on that dreadful night
Without it he could have died or be in a desperate plight.
He was hit from behind and didn't put up a fight
Who they were he didn't get a chance to sight.
To thank you both our family would like to take you out one evening to dine
Any time suitable to you both will be fine."
He left his phone number and away they went
I was surprised and delighted at their intent.

I phoned Jenny and we made a suitable date
We were to be picked up by taxi for our meeting at eight.
It was to the town's smartest hotel that we were invited
We would be on time so the family wouldn't feel slighted.
When we arrived there was no family reception at all!
Just two gentlemen welcoming us—Peter and Paul.
Waiting to accompany us to a dinner and dance
Peter's Mum and Dad will thank us another time when given the chance.

We wined and dined and enjoyed a wonderful dance
It was all so unexpected and left us in a trance.
Peter and Paul then asked us out for another date
When we got home we were in a euphoric state.
A year later we had all tied the wedding knot
Jenny and I were delighted at what we had got.
We still both live close to each other
And reminisce how we each got our lover.

Lady luck, good fortune and fate have been very kind to us
Now we are determined to stay on our happy family bus.

Our Garden of England

The garden of England is the name given to the shire of Kent,
Acclaimed by the locals and visitors, their praise is truly meant.
Blessed with green fields, rivers, valleys, foliage and trees galore
Nurtured by weather providing a climate which does ensure
That the Kentish farmers, on the rich earth do produce a goodly crop.
The green fields, hills and dales allowing sheep and cattle to chew non-stop.

Kent has a coastline which homes many a port,
Giving gardeners and farmers the opportunity their produce to export.
The ports with their trawlers enhance the "The Man of Kent's" diet
Providing the fruits of the sea, whetting everyone's appetite
Our shore is only twenty miles distant from our neighbour France,
For centuries Kent has been a stepping stone into England that visitor's chance.

The Romans invaded Kent, and created the famous Roman Way,
The Normans conquered us, and in Kent came to stay.
These two nations changed the face of our "Olde Worlde" country,
Introduced roads, drainage, buildings, churches, and much more was their bounty.
In the last century because of our position in England, and gateway to the world
In the cause of progress, railways, airports and mighty roads have through our
    countryside swelled.

The Roman Way was the road to London, England's great city
Armies, caravans, pilgrims, the common man, travelled along with alacrity
The great county of Kent is being hauled into a new modern world
Factories, schools, shopping precincts, housing estates are taking over the beauty
    of nature forever spoiled.
The growing world of man his avaricious appetite swallows up our diminishing garden
His need to build and build and build brooks no pardon.

The Garden of Kent not so long ago was nature's home to be sure
Dear God, don't let our Kent be concreted all over and become folk lore.
Look around and discover the fabulous walks of this Kentish shire,
There are still many, satisfying the naturalists every desire.
Roam among the orchards, the vineyards, the wheat fields and listen to the babbling brooks running free
Admire the cattle stock, Kent's fine horses, the shepherds lambs revelling
In the Spring spree.

Admire the wild life that habits our hedgerows, woodlands, river banks and in
    many a tree,
Listen to the glory of the bird life, flying everywhere, flying free.
Listen to the roar of the sea pounding on the shore,
Walk along our sandy beaches which we all adore.
Our Garden of Kent's face is changing every day,
Dear God, Please, Please keep this garden green and beautiful come what may.

When Is It Spring?

Spring is coming, or is it already here?
Global warming has unsettled its seasonal arrival it does appear.
Winter is becoming warmer, less cold, but still very wet,
Winds blow strong and flooding we get.

The warming of our atmosphere and our sacred earth,
Awakens Spring flowers to give early birth.
Encroaching into Winters morbid and dark domain,
Bringing hope and colour into Winter's depressive and sombre reign.

This seasonal shift has brought forth wild primrose, snowdrop,
Camellias, roses, cornflowers, all blossoming in this precocious crop.
Still ever present is lurking the proverbial Jack Frost,
If active, all Spring's forerunners at a stroke would be lost.

If the cycle of life changes its habitual seasonal gear,
The warmer Winter will be detrimental to bird life we hear.
If insects breed ahead of their regular time,
Then birds who depend on them will quickly decline.

Global warming is slowly changing the world as we know it,
Soon all life on earth will be looking for a survival kit.
When the ice-clad mountains, the frozen tundras the glaciers melt,
Another deadly blow against the human race is dealt.
If mankind is creating global warming by his mindless insanity,
Nothing can save the worlds avaricious humanity.

A Journey of Discovery

I have never travelled on a ship or cruised before,
I dream of travelling on an ocean liner soon, opening this exciting door.
I dream of travelling to the shores of sunshine lands,
Of being welcomed by a host of smiling faces and military bands.

I dream of travelling in luxurious comfort and style,
Of being cosseted with great service, excellent food, entertained over every ocean mile.
I dream of watching the golden sunsets before every night fall,
The thrill of my ship entering foreign harbours, my eager spirit to enthral.

I have seen films, read books, devoured any material that comes my way,
I dream to cruise, to discover the world when it becomes my day.
I dream of sailing to find nature's wonders and manmade ones too.
Wouldn't it be wonderful touching the old and feeling the new.

An event such as a cruise should convey joy and goodwill wherever she docks,
Bring out the flags, the bunting, the ladies in their glamorous frocks.
When I hear of new cruisers launching it sets my heart aglow,
I dream that on her bows my voyage of discovery will satisfy my adventurous spirits' ego.

A Sweeping Success

Trevor Brown was 23, the year of nineteen seventy-four
He was out of work that made life a bore.
He was willing to undertake any job or chore.
Disregarding what the future held in store.

His big setback in life—he could not read
Such a handicap if you wish to succeed.
With figures he was very good and sound
But being unable to read he was always downed.

He got a job at last with Tiverton City
Who were not interested in his reading disability.
As long as he was fit and could sweep with agility
That was all they required for their suitability.

After two years in their employ he misheard an important instruction
Caused major upheaval and much disruption.
If being able to read, he could have saved the day
But as he couldn't he was fired straight away.

He lived with his parents who encouraged him to stay
With his savings he bought an impoverished house down the way
The bank manager provided him with a loan for its repair
He plastered, tiled, plumbed and decorated with care.

When finished he had doubled its worth and rented it out
The bank manager was most impressed without a doubt.
Offered to support his next commercial proposition
Which Trevor accepted and brought to successful fruition.

The bank manager supported Trevor for the next year and more
He now had twenty houses, a block of flats and ground rents galore.
The bank manager asked Trevor to visit the bank to discuss
About putting his assets into a limited company without any fuss.

It would make the bank happy and help beat the tax man
He advised Trevor strongly that this was the way forward to plan.
Trevor listened and said as he could not read
He would take advice from his accountant which he would heed.

The bank manager gasped with surprise and said
"Good Gracious, man—you are a millionaire and cannot read
Think what you would be now and what you would have achieved
If you had learnt to read."
Trevor leant forward and slowly tapped his pipe into the ashtray
He said, "Most probably sweeping the King's highway."

The Black Forest

The night was black, the night was still,
The night was silent, the night was chill.
The night was menacing, the night was deep.
The awesome night many odious secrets keep.

The forest is home of the Great Dark Sprite,
This evil goblin thrives in the darkness of the night.
When the dawn rises and begins to appear,
Into the black holes of earth he does disappear.

In the daylight from this evil sprite we need not fear,
In the black of night he is master, never be near.
At night the souls of the damned are tormented and released,
Thousands of years have passed since their lives were deceased.

The sprite, lord of the night, demands more to join his community,
In his dark kingdom he incarcerates with impunity.
In their cottages in front of their log fire,
Elders warn their young, and never tire,
Telling stories of horror and terror that dwell in the dreaded Black Forest,
Keep away and never become the evil goblin's guest.

Rydon and the Motherstone

*(The Tinker is a storyteller who visits Tommy and relates tales of long
ago. He calls late at night just before Tommy goes to sleep.)*

The church clock chimes and midnight comes again,
Staying awake for Tommy is quite a strain.
The problem is Tommy doesn't know if the Tinker is due,
What delight when the Tinker appears and takes a pew.

"Hello, Tommy, glad you are still awake,
If you are ready I will begin to narrate."
Tommy grinned, and whispered, "Please kind, Tinker, go ahead,"
Tommy was ready to absorb every thing the Tinker said.

Many, many years ago, in the Kingdom of Middle Earth
Lived our hero Rydon, aged 22, in the land of his birth.
Rydon was the eldest son of Davrik who was the tribes head
Elected by the tribes' elders, Davrik ruled, counselled and led.

One day in early spring Davrik spoke seriously to his heir
The time has come, on a journey you must travel with the greatest care.
Our Motherstone is nearly 50 years old,
To keep it active, it must be refurbished we are told.

Its nearly 50 years ago our community was presented with this stone
For supporting Thorak the White Wizard in the war against the evil Kraston
We lost over 200 of our men, the price was very dear,
With the stones protection our weakened tribe had little to fear.

24 tribes supported Thorak in the war and when evil was overcome
Thorak with his great power made sure justice was done.
He presented each tribe a Motherstone for their care and protection
Each stone was bonded with the other 23 for unification.

Each stone was a sensor in its own vicinity
Could detect evil and trouble and safeguard each tribes destiny.
They would relay their knowledge to each other stone in their ring
It covered Middle Earth, it created security and made safety their thing.

Each stone was to be reinvigorated within a 50 year span
Thorak the White Wizard made this part of his grand plan.
To keep all the tribes in touch, and united together
So Middle Earth, if threatened, would react to defend themselves at the drop
of a feather.

The time is nigh when our Motherstone must go to the Mount of Orm,
And thrown in to its cavernous fires at the break of dawn.
It's a long journey, you must be full of courage and resolve
You may meet many dangers, but your courage must not dissolve.

The future of your tribe, your loved ones, your kith and kin,
Will depend on you, this race you must win.
The heart of the stone is all you need to take,
Never at any time this stone you will forsake.

This stone you will carry in a pouch close to your heart,
Once strapped on you, you must never be apart.
The stone will tell you if you are in danger, and what you must do,
Whether strangers met are friend or foe, ignore and you will surely rue.

Your trusty sword will be honed on the Motherstone and invoke
A sharpness that will cut anything, or kill at a stroke
Your tunic will be of a natural green
Will change colour when needed, so by your enemy you will not be seen.

Your horse will be the best the tribe can provide
A fine stallion, you make a great pair with you astride.
The mountain of Orm is in the direction of Norse
The stone will guide you if you go off course.

You will be drawn to the abode of Thorak the White
Close by the Mountain of Orm will be in your sight.
Thorak will instruct on what you have to do,
To refresh our Motherstone, and return it to us as new.

Tomorrow, my son, you must be on your way,
On your hazardous path you must not stray.
The responsibility on your shoulders will be great
Your success or failure will decide all our fate.

The Tinker looks at Tommy, says, "The scene is set,
The importance of success you can surely beget
The journey is long, the dangers ahead of which we are unsure
Let's see what happens, what our hero will endure.

At the break of day, our hero mounts his steed and is away,
He will have to ride and ride many a day.
Rydon has 3 months to reach his destination
It allows little lost time and no procrastination

After weeks of relentless galloping, the stone asked Rydon to halt
The request was quite sudden and brought him to a jolt.
Down the valley you must go through, a band of killers lie in wait,
They have been told of your journey and must end your fate.

You must move off this path, and walk through the stream,
Your enemy must not be able your tracks to glean.
Wait two days, your foes will look for you, and pass you by
While waiting, make no smoke, or they will find you, and you will die.

While resting, in a cave with his trusty steed
There appeared a serpent, huge with a hunger need
It sniffed blood and into the cave it went,
With one mighty stroke of his sword, the serpent's life was spent.

Nearing his destination, Rydon ran into a storm
Taking cover for the night under a cliff—this being the norm
Waking in the morning, fallen rock and bush blocked his way
His cutting sword soon cleared the intrusion, and he continued his way.

His next attack came from high in the sky
Two huge vultures fancied him, and decided to eat him or try!
The stone warned him of the hazard, so he dismounted,
Picked his ground where his strength and full skill counted.

The birds could only attack one by one because of Rydon's defensive position
The first bird swooped, missed and received the swords fatal incision.
Realising its last moments had arrived, and fled the fray
Knowing it wasn't going to last the day.

The second vulture, hovered and considered his prey
Then dived swiftly with all force and sway.
Our hero twirled and twirled his sword above his head,
It pierced the great bird's heart and it dropped dead.

Rydon knew time was pressing him to reach his destination
To meet Thorack the White Wizard with his presentation
He galloped and galloped both night and day
Knowing he must arrive on time, come what may.

The stone guided Rydon down to a house in the valley,
Rydon has reached the home of his tribe's greatest ally.
He was met at the door with a great big smile
"Rydon young man, you have done well, travelled many a mile.

Tonight you must rest, tomorrow we visit Mount Orm
Stay here the night and wait for the dawn.
You alone must throw the Motherstone into the eternal fire,
Thereby meeting the needs of your tribe, your loved ones and your desire."

Walking on the side of Mount Orm, Rydon came upon a cave
Striding in, he needed all the breath he could save
The heat from the eternal furnace roared and spluttered a few yards ahead,
Rydon threw with all his might the Motherstone into the fiery bed

A gentle flash exploded, lit up all the cave and its surround
Rydon backed away, out into the open air feeling sound.
He walked back to Throrak sitting on his white horse
"Well done, Rydon, your brave action will help many of course

The heart of the Motherstone you have just placed in the fire
Will be revitalised returned to your tribal home as you desire
When you go home, you must still take great care
You have succeeded in your dangerous mission, an adventure most rare.

You must travel south, and stay on that very line
You will not have the Motherstone, your journey to define
But I give you an Asdic stick, which will guide you if ever in need
Evil Kraston cares not for you now, but all danger you must heed."

Rydon took a longer route to get home cosseting the Motherstone
He travelled back home ward bound, a long way, always alone
Now with his faithful steed he came upon the gates of dear old home
It would be a long time before again, he would want to roam.

The refreshed Motherstone had advised Rydon's tribe of his coming
Everyone stood at the gates cheering; tales of his bravery were humming,

They laid a feast on, to commemorate this great occasion
Rydon was home, their champion, a wonderful reason for an unforgettable
celebration.

The Tinker smiled and said "It is late Tommy, farewell, now I must hurriedly go
Back to my home in the land of long ago.

I Look into Your Face

I look into your face and what do I see
Your love for me, is wondrously obvious as can be,
Your loving eyes, so pure and true,
Your rosy lips, eager to kiss me anew.

I look into your into face and what do I see
My future happiness is around thee.
Until I met you, I did not know the joys of life
Only enhanced when you consented to be my wife.

I look into your face and what do I see
I visualise the future, glorious and free,
You are my purpose you are my adoration
You are truly my inspiration.

I look into your face and what do I see
My future is yours, you hold the key.
We walk hand in hand, into a bright new day,
Our love will conquer the world, come what may.

I look into your face and what do I see
Our union will be forever I plea,
Dear Lord, I acknowledge what a lucky man I am,
Please bless this marriage as only you can.

My Love, My Love

My love, my love you are so far away,
Your absence makes it a long, long day.
I miss your comfort throughout the night,
Your gentle kisses and caresses are always a delight.

Our letters to each other bridge our distant gap,
If two days late my heart goes pit-a-pat.
You say you will be away only four weeks more,
Off the calendar I will tick the days to be sure.

I sit on a seat on top of a hill
Watching the sun disappearing until
I wander slowly home thinking of you,
To dream of when our touching again will renew.

My love, my love you are so far away,
Return to my loving arms without delay.
I want you here with me so very much,
I cant bear to be without your loving touch.

I long to hear you coming through our door,
The man I shall love forevermore.
Now I must wait till you return here
To fill my heart with happiness and cheer.

Enjoy Today While You May

I arise from my bed and draw the curtain
To face a day, of which one is never certain.
What will happen to you or me
Whatever will happen, will be, will be.

I am fortunate to be alive on this earth
In spite of its troubles, its sorrow, its mirth.
I am fit, the key to life,
With it you can overcome trouble and strife.

I look out at the morning dawn
The world sings as another day is born
The heavens chaperone in the glorious sun
Its golden smile betraying warmth and fun.

Today I plan to walk over hill and down
To avoid the madding crowd and busy town.
Wishing to hear the babbling brook
To listen to the song of the mating rook.

To walk all day at a leisurely ramble
To ascend small hillock with gentle scramble.
To stop, listen and admire
To be part of nature's great world out there.

I come to rest on the gentle seashore
Sit and appreciate the wildlife galore.
The birds in their flocks, a glorious sight,
Diving and searching for their daily diet.

Tired and content I am homeward bound
The night moves in without a sound.
'Tis time for me to think of bed
To lay down my weary and happy head.

To dream of a world as it should be
Where nature and civilisation live in harmony.
If we do not learn to live together
This world as we know it, will disappear forever.

My Wishing Well

At the bottom of my garden is a little wishing well,
How long it has been there I cannot tell.
It was there when I was very small,
Three feet 'round, with a low brick wall.

When active, it was ten feet deep
Clear fresh water it did keep.
Rising from an underground basin I am told,
Its contents always pure and rather cold.

Then Mother Nature changed her way
Our well has not seen water for many a day.
The rope and bucket have gone long ago
Now it stands still and forlorn, that's so.

For many years, perhaps a score or more
It has become my wishing well, just as in folklore.
When I want my dreams to become real
Into the garden at night I quietly steal.

Beneath the moon with its round face
Willing me from outer space
To drop my gift into the wishing well
Praying it will grant me a magic spell.

My mother taught me never to be greedy,
Help others, especially the needy,
And your rewards will flow back,
Happiness and contentment you will rarely lack.

Once, visiting the well with its friendly appeal
I asked it to make my mother heal.
I feel sure I gave it a gentle nudge
To cure a malady that would not budge.

My little well and I through out our past
Have a bonding that will last
In this sceptic world, all is not what it may seem,
A childhood romance made a little well more than just a dream.

Enjoy Your Life

Count your blessings, not your woes
Count your friends, be benevolent to your foes.
Count your courage, forget your fears
Count your smiles, wash away your tears.
Count your good health, work hard to stay fit
Count your determination, maintain your true grit.
Count your marriage and make it work through
Count your children as your blessing too.
Count your happiness, indeed you are a lucky man
Be positive, smile, enjoy life as only you can.

The Other Side of the Rainbow

Where is the other side of the rainbow?
Tell me, guide me, take me, that's where I want to go.
When I see its beauty radiant in the sky
I want to leap from my wheelchair and fly high.

I have given up dreaming of walking down the street,
Running races, I will never be able to compete.
On the other side of the rainbow I am told,
No one is disabled or ill, what a place to behold.

On warm days I would run down to the sea,
I would swim and splash with glee, with glee, with glee.
Unless you have been wrapped up in a wheelchair like me,
You will never truly know how much I long to be free.

To walk in the valleys and enjoy the closeness of Mother Nature,
Thrill to the galaxy of flowers, shrubs and trees presenting a glorious picture.
If lucky I have another thirty years to live on Earth I know,
But my heart beckons me to the Land of the Rainbow to go.

I am not complaining about my life on this good earth,
I was born with my disability at birth.
They say think positive and always have a dream.
I pray that some one in heaven will shoot down a beam
And transport me to the Land of the Rainbow,
Where I will walk tall, run free, be happy, I know, I know, I know.

The Owl and the Fox Go Hunting

The full moon shone brightly that night,
In the open fields there was shed much light.
The fox sat silent and still in the trees shadow,
The owl perched high on the branch motionless, another predatory fellow.

Both waiting and watching for the unsuspecting prey,
Into the killing fields they hope will stray.
A hedgehog snuffles into this potentially dangerous scene,
Both predators know with its spikes there is no meal here to glean.

A rabbit pops up out of its warren,
The owl knows to strike now, so that its brood that night will not go barren.
With its silent swift and deadly speed
With a ghost-like *swoop* his talons seize the prey ensuring his family will feed.

Reynard decides in these conditions he cannot compete,
Trawling the river banks, the woods, the farmer's yard to capture his treat,
That is the direction he must surely go,
To return empty handed to his den would indeed be a tale of woe.

He rises, trots into the gloomy wood, his tread as light as a feather,
Our cunning friend will eat almost anything whether
It be fish, bird animal or insect, come what may,
The more wholesome, the more appetites he will allay.

The vixen and cubs are waiting in their den,
Hoping to feast on a fat juicy hen.
Our predator only visits the farm when he is in a desperate state,
Wary of the farmer's gun and other risks he must take.

Tonight he has eaten two mice, three eggs and a few snails,
On many foraging expeditions he will catch enough, or unfortunately fail.
Tonight Reynard has caught only a few small prey.
Tomorrow Reynard and family sincerely hope it will be a much better day.

The Girl That I Marry

It was around eighteen that I began to look at girls with interest,
Mum had advised me when marrying I should put the girls to this test.
It was important that they could cook for you and family,
Bear children and rear them to ensure the family tree.

To be able to sew and darn will be another attribute,
To be able to soothe my troubled brow, always be pretty and cute.
Love the children, but keep them under a firm hand,
You must love each other with every fibre and strand.

All this I took to heart when seeking for a wife,
To bring me joy, contentment and happiness for the rest of my life.
What actually happened I met this beautiful girl at a dance,
I immediately fell in love, I did not have a chance.

That was three months ago, tomorrow I am to be wed
All my mother's advice has never entered my head.
My heart never ruled caution, I fell madly in love instead.
My heart was so happy, all reason has fled.
My mother has blessed our union and said,
"If you have married the right woman all will be well,
And happiness and comfort for you and your family in your home will forever dwell."

There Is a Time...

There is a time to bed, and a time to dine
There is a time to venture, and a time to follow the line
There is a time to party, and a time to pray
There is a time to work, and a time to play
There is a time to agree, and a time to have your say
There is a time to fight, and a time to walk away
There is a time to sell, and a time to buy
There is a time to relax, and a time to try
There is a time to speak, and a time to hear
There is a time to hate, and a time to love most dear
There is a time to run free, and a time to accept responsibility
There is a time to be intelligent, and a time to show naivety
In this world life is short, always smile and do your bit
The world will be a better place if you stand up and never quit.

Zing

The get up and goers in this world need zing,
One of the greatest instigators of this energy is spring.
It revitalises the world from its winter sleep,
It sorts out the men from the boys, the goats from the sheep.

Spring is the time when your heart beats faster,
You must absorb its rhythm and become its master.
When spring arrives the whole world moves up a gear,
Every go-getter will plan out an exciting and fruitful year.

Spring sets alight the touch paper to fire our minds,
We explore and venture into new situations of all kinds.
Yes, of course we work and plan all the year round,
But it is in spring we jump, leap and bound.

Spring throughout the life of man has given him zing.
Spring creates new birth with all living things.
Spring brings hope, inspiration and makes the world sing,
The world progresses, moves on, because we are instilled with zing.

I Want to Be a Poet

I want to be a poet
Whose verse will please all those who hear or read.
I want to be a poet
To stir passions, encourage and raise hopes of those in need.
I want to be a poet
Write about joy and love and what happiness it will bring.
I want to be a poet
Write about poverty, wealth, the man who would be king.
I want to be a poet
Write about history and visions of the future.
I want to be a poet
Write about good and evil, the wicked and the pure.
I want to be a poet
Write about King Arthur and his band of knights.
I want to be a poet
Write about everything and common sights.
I want to be a poet
Putting the magical word and phrase together.
I want to be a poet
To dream my verse will be enjoyed forever and ever.
I want to be a poet
No one can convey everything, action, deed, love or disaster but I will try,
I will try, I will try until the day I die.

When She Loves Me…?

When she loves me I feel like a king,
When she loves me not, I wonder if I have done a wrong thing.
When she loves me I feel confident and great,
When she loves me not I get into a state.
When she loves me I feel I am walking on air,
When she loves me not, I am full of despair.
When she loves me I respond and smile, smile, smile,
When she loves me not, I leave home and run a mile.
When she loves me I feel the world is sunny and good,
When she loves me not, I would put anything right if I could.
When she loves I remember our shared joys with delight,
When she loves me not, I keep in the shadows well out of sight.
When she loves me I will dance and sing,
When she loves me not I wonder what other problems the day will bring.
Fortunately she loves me most of the time,
When she does not, I have leant to stay cool and toe the line.
When she loves me again I feel fine,
I do so love her and I want her to remain forever mine.

A Pile of Ballyhoo

The old lady was pulled up by the police—driving too fast.
When the officer asked for her driving licence she looked aghast,
She replied" Sorry officer, I haven't got one, it was taken from me
Four years ago, I was involved in a drunken spree."
The officer asked her for her vehicle registration or log book.
"It's not my car, Officer, it's stolen, I needed a car so I took
this car from a back street near to me
I had the urge to drive and feel free."

"Unfortunately, Officer, I ran over and killed a man,
Stuffed him into my boot, had to hide him as quickly as I can.
Taking him down to the river to drop him in plop
Sadly I have now been caught by a speed cop."
The officer panicked, he had got a dangerous woman here
Must get help in case she blows her top.
The officer rang head office to get back up if he can
A short while later an inspector arrived with six men armed to the teeth was every man.

The inspector said to the old lady, "Step out of the car, please."
She said, "Is there anything wrong, Officer, you don't seem at ease."
He requested, "Open up the boot of your car so we can see
What you have in there." It was as empty as can be.
"Madam, where are your registration papers so we can see who this car belongs to."
"Here they are, Officer, its mine," producing the documents without any ado.
"Finally, let me see your driving licence if I may."
The inspector was getting totally confused, it was not his best day.

She produced her driving licence, smiled and sweetly said
"Tell me, Officer, what is all this about, I want to go home to bed."
"Madam, I apologise, but one of my officers had informed me
That you had no driving licence, no vehicle registration and there was a dead
body in the car trunk."
"Obviously, Officer, as you can see all of this was a load of bunk
I bet he told you that I was speeding too
To add to this complete nonsense—a total pile of ballyhoo!"

Four Empty Chairs

Four empty chairs sit in the warm evening sun
The family is away at the seaside having fun.
Set around a bubbling and sparkling waterfall
The evening shadows fall long and tall.

The grass well cut, the flowers in orderly array
The trees at their greenery best, keeping autumn at bay
Put a finishing touch to a lovely scene
But the four empty chairs—what do they mean?

The missing sound of noise and laughter
Of children playing and fighting and looking after
The other child's toys which are not theirs
Of kitten and dog chasing up and down stairs.

The gardener with mower, rake, hoe and spade
Will despair when he sees the damage made
By enthusiastic children and their energetic intent,
Pets playing with each other to their hearts' content.

Every house needs a family to make it a home
When they are away it sits like a desolate dome
A home needs like a woman, to be spoilt and adored
It needs life and attention, into it happiness poured.

When you my love and the family are here
I relax, enjoy and become full of cheer.
To me our home will never be complete,
Until you all return and each take your seat.

Peter the Lover

Peter loved the ladies, Peter loved them all,
Peter loved as many as he could enthral,
Peters adage was God made me as I am,
So I love all the ladies as I can.

Peter married early on in life,
At twenty four had three children and a forgiving wife.
After working in the office all day
The family hardly saw him as he was always on an amorous foray.

Peter always had four relationships on the go,
With well-to-do unmarried ladies, he did not want husbands as foe.
He spread his charm and masculinity around as far as was able,
He never encouraged the fair sex who wanted someone stable.

For ten years his long suffering wife put up with this façade,
Of Peter being Jack the Lad and an amorous cad.
Life is full of twists and turns, of ups and downs
Meeting new loves with smiles, departing with tears and frowns.

One of his disappointed amours would not let him go,
Was not going to let anyone else have him, that was so,
As he was saying farewell in his usual charming way,
Ignoring the desperate ladies plea to stay,
This past ladylove decided no one else would share his bed,
She pulled out a gun and shot him dead.

In the heavens above God studied Peter's history and lifestyle,
Endeavouring to make ladies happy for a short while,
Then leaving them bereft, sad and in despair
Seeking further self gratification in yet another affair.

God decided Peter should serve as a eunuch in a harem,
Not exactly what Peter prayed for it would seem.
The Good Lord decreed that Peter would be castrated,
Making sure his future amorous intentions would be frustrated.

Grounds for Divorce

Mrs. Murphy went to see the best solicitors in town,
They were called Grogan, Paddiwick and Brown.
Mrs. Murphy decided it was time to get a divorce,
She was positive she could find justifiable grounds of course.

She made her appointment with an elderly Mr. Brown,
Experienced in these matters, he was renowned.
Question one he asked" Does Mr. Murphy beat you on your body or head?"
"Not likely," she replied. "If he did, I would kill him stone dead."

Question two he asked, "Does he keep you short of money," "Not at all"
She replied, "Every Friday night he fills my purse, always on the ball."
Question three, "Do you know if he has ever been unfaithful to you?"
Mrs. Murphy responded with a smile, "I can tell you true
I think we have grounds for divorce, I will tell you why,
He did not father my last child and that's no lie!"

Awake, My Love

It is morning I lie awake
My love sleeps beside me
I need him to my passion slake
It is a day when we are both free.

We have been married just a year
We have our own little flat
We both have to work hard at top gear
To pay the bills arriving on our doormat.

My love works five nights a week
I work in an office during the day
When he comes home he doesn't seek
To make love, he is tired, not at peak.

At weekends and holidays we bond together
I must always be at my best
I want our marriage to last forever and ever
Our love and passion ensure our union is no jest.

I gently nudge my love and remind him I am here
I want to be loved, caressed and wooed
I will tell him he is my most precious dear
That he is not my fancy man or dude.

He awakes, I cannot resist that adoring smile
He kisses me, I am again in Heaven
It is going to be a wonderful day
And it's only just half past seven!

The Homecoming

I have returned to England from the land of the didgeridoo
The land of the kangaroo, and there are quite a few.
For forty years I have lived in the Aussie Outback
Rearing sheep, shearing the wool off their back.

For the first ten years our home was a wooden shack
Every amenity, especially water, we did lack.
All my life my favourite colour was green,
In this part of the world it was rarely seen.

For my dear wife Edna life was a long chore
What kept her going was our son Tom whom we both did adore.
He was educated sixty miles away
He boarded at the schools, at weekends he came home to stay.

Then he won a university scholarship in biology
It meant he would go to England to continue his study.
There he achieved his degrees, a fellowship, and a loving wife
He became successful, had a family, enjoyed life.

We missed him as any parent would
He had his own life to make we clearly understood.
A few months ago Edna suddenly became very sick
We quickly got her into hospital, but that didn't do the trick.

She passed away in a deep sleep with little or no pain
Losing my love there was no reason to remain,
Alone in the Outback, my neighbour the desert plain
Then I heard the most welcome refrain.

Tom and family offered me a home with them and retire
I gladly accepted, to return to England was always my desire.
I am now 74, have family love, share a warm home
Till my days run out I shall not be alone.
My homecoming will only be truly complete
When Edna and I sit together again on our divine seat.

Harvest Time

I remember as a country lad when I lived in the village of Little Carlton,
It was harvest time that demanded everyone's attention.
All prayed the harvest would be good,
Each prayed when harvesting started the sun would shine as it should.

When it came to the cutting of the wheat, the barley and the rye,
Blue skies, bright and dry days would set our hopes on high.
The men with sickle and scythe would cut through out the long day,
The women folk would provide sustenance and support all the way.

Behind the men the ladies would bundle and stack,
The elders and children would join in and bend their back.
They brought in the wagon cart and two horses to carry the grain,
Back to the barn where throughout the winter it would remain.

The fruits of the season could be picked in a more relaxed way,
Apples, pears, berries each in turn held their sway.
Everyone joined in to glean the crops and pack them too,
To ensure they would keep in good condition the whole winter through

It was the gathering of the harvest that kept the villagers all together,
They pulled as a united team whatever the weather.
The harvest would be the result of a hard years toil,
Sowing the seed, cultivating, extracting the most from the Earth's precious soil.

When it came to the Harvest Festival and the blessing in the house of the lord,
Everyone came to celebrate, give thanks, each on their own accord.
A successful harvest would make all the villagers hearts glad,
It meant in winter, food on the table, coal in the hearth, and folk well clad.

Then we had three bad years when the crops were poor,
That was when poverty and disaster came knocking on our door.
We had no alternative but to look for work in another place,
Dad's brother ran a small factory in the Midlands that made lace.

He offered us shelter, provided Mum, Dad and me a job too.
We would all have to reorganise our lives and learn many things anew.
It's three years now we have lived in Buxton Town, Dad's brother has been kind,
Helped us settle in, always obliging, nothing a bind.
My family and I know we shall stay here the rest of our days,
But nothing will ever replace our happy memories of harvesting and the country ways.

The Traveller from Where?

It was autumn, through my cottage window I watched the sun setting,
The weather signs for tomorrow, another fine day we would be getting.
There was a chill in the air now the heat of the day was gone,
I put two small logs on the fire indicating my day was nearly done.

I moved to put out the candles which took the place of the fading twilight,
When extinguished I would bed for the night.
Suddenly there was a *tap tap* on the door,
I thought, *O God my neighbour's in trouble to be sure,*

I opened the door, in the dusk there stood a seasoned man.
He looked tall, well travelled, and with a weathered tan.
Nervously I said, "What can I do for you?"
With an infectious grin he replied, "A piece of bread, a jug of ale, a night in
your barn would do."

I invited him in and asked him to sit by the hearth,
For a few days stay here I could earn my keep he said with a laugh.
The fire sprang up, with his presence the house became suddenly warm,
I liked my visitor, his charm stopped me feeling alone, depressed and forlorn.

Living by myself I always lack news of the world outside,
Now I could learn something if my traveller awhile did abide.
"Yes I could put you up tonight, longer if you need,
You can sleep here by the fire or in the barn if you so agreed."

On the table was a loaf made fresh yesterday,
My neighbour's wife baked bread and scones and delivered every fourth day.
I sliced the loaf, cut some cheese and poured a jug of ale,
I had a gut feeling this stranger could tell many a tale.

"My name is Duncan, I depend on the world being kind,
I travel the country, not knowing what I shall find,
Sometimes I can help by listening to an appealing call,
Other times I can heal, advise, preventing a disastrous downfall."

At dawn we rose washed and fed.
We went to see Barney my sheepdog sick on his bed,
A thorn had entered and poisoned his front paw,
It had swollen tremendously, it looked ugly and sore.

Duncan examined the infestation and said "This we must urgently treat,
Bring me hot water if this infection we are to beat,"
He blended herbs into a steamy brew,
Bathed gently at length, and in the evening this treatment he did renew.

I did not realise that Barney had been at deaths door,
Our traveller had saved his life and his health did restore.
Duncan worked with me and did what I asked him to,
Sometimes improving on the way every day jobs I do.

Duncan stayed five days and nights, a great benefit was he,
His quiet friendly presence was an uplift for me.
In our breaks during the day and in the evenings too,
He told me about the outside world, what was happening, what was new.

On the last night we were preparing to go to bed
"Toby, I have a message to give to you," he said
"When I was travelling around I entered a church to pray, as I often do,
I had a vision, a command, to come and visit you.

Mary your loved one and departed wife in the heavens above,
Said she misses you and sends her love,
Enjoy your life in full, and when you are ready to come,
She will be waiting to greet you in the setting of the sun.

I was totally surprised, said, "Thank you," and crept upstairs to sleep,
Remembering Mary and the happy times we shared made me weep.
When I arose at dawn, Duncan had already departed,
Left me a farewell note, told me to keep cheerful and do not get down hearted.

On the table was a wedding ring, one that Mary had worn,
It had been put there by Duncan, its presence made me feel good, I felt reborn.
I put it on a chain around my neck, wore it close to my heart,
Until death, we two shall not part.

I return to Duncan, my visitor who came from, I know not where?
Who enhanced my life, saved my precious dog Barney, was full of care.
Why should this occurrence happen to me?
It was a miracle that was plain to see.
Duncan left me with a ring that came from the grave of my beloved wife,
Left me meditating if there is in the hereafter another life?
Dear Duncan, from where ever you come from, who ever you may be
Your visit will always be a wonderment to me!!

Promises, Promises, Promises

A promise is for something near or far,
A promise can offer success or your future to mar.
A promise can be a spur to get you going,
A promise can inspire you to put on your best showing.
A promise can be the cause of you being sad,
A promise can be the cause of you being glad.
A promise is in the mind of what will be,
A promise does not guarantee any certainty.
A promise of reward makes men work to excess,
A promise can make a man eager to his lady to impress.
A promise to mankind can encourage his best endeavour,
A promise of joy and happiness will vitalise his vigour.
A promise in our lives is a very important thing,
A promise we pray will to you happiness bring.
A promise can make us think positive and the future to behold,
A promise can determine whether we act weak or bold.
A promise can mean so much to us all,
On a promise we can all rise or fall.

The Swans

One of my joys is to go walking along our river banks,
Beset with trees and green fields, to nature we give our thanks.
In summer the river runs deep, slow and serene,
Under the shade of a willow I can sit and dream.

I settle down and behold the ripples on the waters top,
In the shallows fish leap to catch water fly on the hop.
In a short while this is over, and the tranquil river progresses smoothly on,
Then a vision glides slowly into sight and my heart is gone.

Two enchanting swans adorned in glorious white feather,
Cooling in summer, keeping the cold at bay in the winter weather.
For many, many years I have chosen to come here,
These plumed beauties have brought me countless moments of great cheer.

In the past I have seen them bring up families of cygnets,
The young ones grow up, mature, and swim away to make another home without regrets.
I wonder how much longer it will be that I will have the pleasure of the swans company?
Their stature and elegance afford me such harmony.
I pray every spring when they return here to their summer place
That we shall enjoy each others pleasure forever with amity and grace.

The Land of Long Ago

Once upon a time in the land of long ago
Everyone was friends, there was no enemy or foe.
In the land of long ago
The sun always shone, no cold winds did blow.
In the land of long ago
Everyone was kind, and happiness did flow.
In the land of long ago
Everyone was good, so the Devil's influence couldn't grow.
In the land of long ago
All the nations sang in one voice—it was a great show.
In the land of long ago
Everyone was equal, no upstairs or stairs below.
In the land of long ago
The expectations of life made everyone's heart glow.
In the land of long ago
The pace of life was leisurely, gentle and more slow.
In the land of long ago
Schools were friendly places, teaching love and all you need to know.
In the land of long ago
If you met a stranger he would always smile and give you a warm hello.
In the land of long ago
Everyone was sincerely interested in you and yours, never shallow.
If this idyllic world ever existed and I hope it was so
Then I wish I had lived in this wonderful world of the
LAND OF LONG AGO.

The Didgeridoo

In the dark of the night the steady drone of the Didgeridoo
Vibrates throughout the entire land of the Kangaroo.
The Aborigines are clacking their clapsticks together in celebration
To rhythms composed by their most ancient and revered generation.

On the hard earth the stamping of the feet
Encourages all to join in with its bewitching beat.
The chanting mesmerises one and all
To be enthralled by its magical call.

The moon and the stars witness this ritual event
The constant droning of the Didgeridoos does not relent.
On this ancient earth when life all began
The Didgeridoos were created by primitive man.
Today to the Aborigine it is a great part of his inheritance
The Didgeridoos will always be a treasure their life to enhance.

Thomas Had Nowhere to Go

It was ten years ago Thomas lost his job as a skilled maintenance man,
His employer upset a large customer, sacked Thomas who took the can.
Living in a small village where most of the work centred around "His Lordship's Estate"
At the age of forty-six, he could not find work at any rate.
All his life he had lived with his parents in a cottage called the Retreat,
Sadly they had passed away many years ago, their divine fathers to meet.
The lass he had fancied when younger, took another lover,
Thomas could not put it to his mind to marry any other.
He had lost his job, the quarterly rent would soon be due.
No income, no family ties, no money, soon no home, he decided he must move on
and make a fresh life anew.

It was nearly July, Berwick Town was thirty miles away
Going now Thomas would be there before the harvesting took sway.
There could be many weeks work to help him on his way.
When the harvest was in there may be thatching, fencing, ditching and carpentry work on offer.
His experience, skill and strength he would be able to competently proffer.
He bade farewell to all his friends who wished him good luck
In spite of being out of work they thought he had a lot of pluck.
On his wheelbarrow Thomas placed all the worldly goods he did own
His working clothes, a tattered Bible, his precious tools and a honing stone.

He packed bread and cheese to sustain him on the road to Berwick Town
Two blankets to keep him warm when sleeping in the open on the ground.
Thomas completed his journey in under five days, the weather had been fair,
On arrival he made his way to the town square.
Within the hour he was approached by a farmer who had a large farm,
Who offered work, three meals a day, accommodation in a closed barn
Thomas proved by initiative a strong arm, agreeability to hard work
When put in charge his responsibility he did not shirk.
Mr. Thenneck, the farmer, impressed by Thomas' output and capability
Offered Thomas a permanent job and a cottage of pleasing suitability.

Thomas could not believe his good fortune and gratefully accepted
Such an opportunity could not be easily rejected.
Two years after settling in and becoming part of the neighbourhood
At a harvest festival party and dance he met Betty, a widow who would
Marry him and for eight years make his life blissfully good.
They were happy and compatible and loved each other as married folk should.
Then a virus struck the area, many took ill and died
Thomas lost Betty, his great grief and sorrow he could not hide.
Mr. Thenneck, now elderly, was taken through death's door
Tragedy had struck Thomas twice hard and soon there would be more.
Mr. Thenneck's heirs were townsfolk who lived far away and were very poor,
They decided to sell the farm and get a good price,
To eke out their old days and live in comfort would be nice.
The farm was sold to a Scotsman with five sons and their clan
Who sacked all the farm workers, took over their cottages, that was his plan.
Thomas with few possessions and little money found himself alone on the open road,
There would be no place of welcome, whichever way he strode.

At his age, with strength failing fast, who would offer him work,
He was prepared to undertake the most menial duties, nothing to shirk.
He ended up as a gardener-cum-handyman, his room a garden shed,
Some cushions, a worn-out old settee was his bed.
His meals, usually leftovers and scraps in the staff kitchen he was fed.
Then disaster struck again, the children of the house burnt down his shed.
Having nowhere to sleep he was told to move on.
In the fire he lost everything that to him did belong.
That night without blankets he laid down in the park to sleep,
His appointment with tomorrow he did not keep.
That night Thomas died of cold in a dark and lonely place,
When they found him, he had a big smile on his tired and gaunt face.
Some say he had found peace at last and had been welcomed to God's heavenly place.

The Telegram

It was the fourth of October, the year was 1944
England and Germany were in bitter conflict fighting a great war.
On that day the dreaded telegram came
After the postman had been life for me and the family would never be the same.

"The Government regrets to inform you that Mr. M. Peters has been killed in action."
Every loved one, kith or kin, prays this reality would only be fiction.
I always believed and prayed this would not happen to my family and me
What our future without husband and dad we couldn't imagine how it would be.

A few days ago, he loved, he laughed, watched the setting of the sun
No more, no more, no more, his life is ended by an enemy gun.
He does forever sleep
Leaving me and my boys to anguish and to weep.

To protect our homeland, our freedom, our treasured democracy
To protect us from the horror of the Nazi boot and German tyranny.
That was why our gallant soldiers went to war
To bring back sanity to the world and peace restore.

No more, no more, no more will Michael weed the garden or mow the grass
Take the family to church to partake in Mass.
There would be a funeral, no body to cremate
The priest would give his sermon, the congregation would mourn, their fondest
Memories to relate.

I thank God that Michael's parents lived close by
Their great support and love kept me rational I could not deny.
I took up War work in a factory to earn our family keep
I had no time for my departed loved one for to weep.

Peace has come now we can sleep safely in our bed
And look to planning our boys' future that lies ahead.
I owe it to my family to continue life as before,
The day the telegram came we will all remember for evermore.

Our Conservatory

To some, glass conservatories are a joy or a bore,
It really depends what you use them for.
On their position, relating to your house and the sun,
Whether used as an indoor garden, a kiddies playroom or for fun.

To the older generation it can be a place of rest,
Looking into the garden, watching the birds at their best.
To some, the conservatory becomes an extra room,
In goes the junk, the whatnot stand, or broken broom.

Our conservatory is twenty feet long and ten feet deep,
Shuts out the cold and the suns warmth it does keep.
Most of the year it provides a pleasant atmosphere,
Helping to dispel dull wet days with a warming cheer.

Yes, sometimes it can become very hot,
We just close our inner doors, so uncomfortable we are not.
We enjoy relaxing in our house of glass,
It has become a blessing we would not pass.

Henry Was True

Henry, Peter and John arrived at Heavens Pearly Gates,
God stood there to decide each of their fates.
God said to Henry, "To your wife have you ever been untrue?"
"Many times I have been tempted," Henry replied. "Being unfaithful neither
Mary or I would ever do."

God said, "Good, for that you can drive around in a Rolls Royce whilst you
are here."
God said to Peter, "To your wife have you ever been untrue, you must answer
honest and clear."
Peter replied, "I am only a man, on rare occasions I have had a bit on the side."
God said, "For being honest around Heaven in a Ford Motor you can ride."

Turning to John the same question did he ask,
Who replied, "In the glory of faithfulness I do not bask,
I love my wife, and all the ladies when I can,
In doing that I believe I am satisfying the ladies according to nature's plan."

God said, "Because of your unfaithfulness I can only award
You with a self propelled skating board."
A month later John was skating around on his board,
When he saw Henry standing by his Rolls Royce, tears from his eyes poured.

John stopped, went over to our Henry and said, "Oh dear,
Why are you crying in Heaven, you have nothing to fear?"
Henry replied, "All my life, however tempted, to my marriage vows I have
always been true,
Now in Heaven I have just seen my wife riding a skate board like you."

The Ominous Fog

The fog rolls in from a heavy sea,
The fog rolls in, the swell is high, the sea choppy.
It covers the shore, shrouding every vessel afloat,
Fishing for the sailor today will be remote.

Today the mariners will be land bound,
A chance to repair nets and make hulls sound.
Cleaning the craft with a good scrub,
The sooner done, the sooner to the pub.

A thick fog is always a sailor's despair
In it loss of life and ship travel as a pair.
Many a ship and crew lie in the ocean's bottom deep,
Ships wrecked on unseen rocks, are now permanently asleep.

Sailors and kinfolk respect the fog and its fearful hand,
History confirms when it is in attendance stay on land.
Today in our small port the lighthouse is the shining star
Warning shipping of our dangerous rocks, near and far.

A gentle breeze from the inland starts to blow,
After a few hours its success starts to show.
The fog on this occasion has met its master,
We all wish it would depart a little faster!

The first good signs, our returning fishing smacks appear
Out of the evening gloom and dock here.
They report the sea of fog, is nearly clear,
Out going sailors eagerly prepare their gear.

On the flowing tide the hungry fishermen sail,
In a week's time they will return to tell their tale.
A sailor's life can be hazardous, he must take care,
In his lifetime every sailor will have to dare.

He must work the seas in weather bad or fair,
Due diligence and respect in his mind, always there,
He is forever at the mercy of fogs and Mother Nature
Only in her benevolence lies every sailor's future.

Patch, My Old Chum

I had a scruffy dog, when clean, he was white!
Skinny and lanky, always hungry, always looking for a bite.
He scoffed down two meals a day, and chewed a bone,
When fed, preferred company, didn't like being alone.
Born with a patch over his right eye,
That got him his name one would not deny.
He became my chum when he was two years old,
Picked him up from a dog's home, he looked ragged and cold.

My first three months with Patch drove me to despair,
He covered everything with his dropping hair.
I explained the situation to our local vet,
Who gave Patch some pills and lotion that made his hair set.
During our first two months together two pairs of slippers did vanish
Those foot comforts I was not going to replenish
Until their whereabouts I could establish,
When proven, the culprit I would banish.

A few weeks later they were found buried at the end of the garden,
Though I growled his large brown eyes wrung out my pardon.
Our evening walks brought us both great pleasure,
He would race about and I strolled at my leisure.
It was when he had spent all his youthful energetic force,
He would cosset me to love him of course.
There was no one else in my life, who gave me such affection,
Ensured we became great pals, that needed no detection.

It was Sunday afternoons I enjoyed the most,
When we had time to visit our local coast.
Patch always made a beeline to dip in the sea,
When finished he would shake himself all over me.
For many years I took a ball for me to throw,
Eagerly he would chase it, slow or quick, high or low.
At the age of sixteen Patch became very poorly,
The vet could not cure him, I was going to miss him sorely.

It was in the garden, in his basket he passed away,
I remember it well, it was a beautiful autumnal day.
As I looked at his shaggy body as he lay,
I felt content that while on earth he enjoyed his stay.
Patch had come to mean so much to me
Now he had gone to meet his maker and run free.
I buried him in the garden under the Lilac tree,
Patch, my old chum you were the best thing that ever happened to me!

The Setting of the Sun

Now I am gone, bid me farewell
For on this good earth I no longer dwell.
My goodbyes to you are sent from the heart,
It pains that we must part.

Our love has lasted for many years now,
For your devotion to the family I can only bow.
Thank you for giving us all such happiness,
Without it, our lives would be sad and dreary, no less.

Mourn awhile for me, grieve if you will
Your depleted life will again soon refill.
Life goes on, your love and care is what the world needs,
Your wisdom and happiness, your loved ones will heed.

I won't be far away, take your time before you come
To join me to watch the setting of the sun.
Listening to music, that whiled away many a happy day,
Waiting for you, what more can I say.

First complete the part of life you will play,
Keep fit, think positive, make every day a great day.
Laugh and the world laughs with you, treasure your smile
When you join me it will be in style.

The world will honour you my darling wife
For all the happiness you have given to me, the family, to the world
throughout your life.

My Mother Told Me…

My mother told me the following story
Relayed to her in her wedding oratory
Just before her wedding day
Keep your marriage blessed, come what may.

Keep telling your loved one "I love you true"
And act that way whatever you do.
It's the woman that makes the union a success
It's the woman who sorts out the problems or mess.

A most important word is *We*
Try not where possible to think of you or me.
Especially when you start the family tree
And pray the Lord is gracious to thee.

It's your spirit in the home that will keep it bright
It's your care that will help the family to unite.
Make the family home a haven and a resting place
Providing love, security, privacy and freedom of space.

God made woman for children to bear
It brings her the greatest happiness and many a tear.
Woman is born to bond with a mate
Her partner's love and cohesion will determine their fate.
Go now in love and put on your nuptial ring
May your hearts forever joyously sing.

What a Newspaper Can Do!

Midday I arrived at my local railway station,
Boarded the two-fifteen according to my expectation.
I entered a carriage with one other gent,
I got out my book and started to read with intent.

The train had been travelling for fifteen minutes or more,
When my travelling companion took out his newspaper and tore
Out a large piece of it and walked over to the carriage door,
Rolled down the window, tossed out the paper, I did not know what for.

He went back to his seat and sat down again,
We both continued to read, relaxing to the rhythm of the train.
Fifteen minutes later he looked at his watch and did it all over again,
Tossed out some paper, and turning, looked at me in distain.

Rather surprised I felt awkward and said nothing,
Wondering if he was just a silly old muffin.
Fifteen minutes later he opened the carriage window wide,
Tossed out more newspaper, this time I could not take it in my stride.

I accosted him and demanded to know
What he thought he was doing throwing out paper so,
He replied, "I am frightening the elephants, keeping them off the railway line."
I thought about it and its logic I could not define.
I went to the window, looked out left and right,
There was not an elephant in sight,
I told him this and he replied, "It just proves what I am doing is right!"

Thank You

Does it seem so long ago when everyone was so polite,
When one would meet, smile, gossip, life was a delight.
One would request with "Please" as you had your say,
And when parting, again smile, and leave with a "Good Day."

I know the pressure of life has dramatically quickened,
When I hear the present day talk and chatter, I sicken.
The swear words, abruptions, mispronunciations purporting to be the Queen's English,
I feel sure a few reprimands would not go amiss.

My parents taught me how to get the best response and respect,
Watch your manners, do not people's feelings neglect.
When they do well or a good job for you,
Praise them and thank them, that will cheer them up too.

If you are disappointed, find something to praise first,
Then gently admonish, only scold at the worst.
The chances are they will want to please you
And try again, and do the best they can do.

The words "Please" and "Thank you" even at this present time,
Will make your life more pleasant and sublime.
People like to be praised and thanked, it only takes a few words,
Do it genuinely, with a smile, you will find Mum's advice wasn't absurd.

Music in the Air

The sun is shining, there is music in the air
My loved one proposed that we make a married pair.
I am so happy, there is music in the air.
I want to dance, sing, tell everybody everywhere,
I must tell my parents, my friends, there is music in the air.
Last night Lee gave me a beautiful engagement ring,
There is music in the air, how my heart is throbbing.
It is planned I shall become a June bride,
Waiting that long I do not know how I will abide.
Lee my fiancé like me is over the moon,
Taking our wedding nuptial vows will never be too soon.
Now I must calm down, move back into the sedentary
way of life,
Always planning how I am going to be a happy and a good wife.
There is music in the air, There is music in the air,
There is music everywhere.

Precious Rain

Rain bouncing on the pavement, running down the street
Creating puddles to drench our careless feet.
Rain splashing on the windows, splashing on the doors,
When it's heavy see how it pours.
Rain running off the roof, running along the gutter,
Running free and fast, only a blocked drain will make it stutter.

Rain filling our ever thirsty garden water butt,
Needed for our floribunda whatever their cut.
Rain when it comes keeps our streams alive,
They run into our rivers so that they may thrive.
Rain in winter accompanied by a dull day
Encourages me in my comfortable home to stay.

I remain indoors, light the fire, draw my curtain,
Waiting for the rain to stop, until of that I am certain.
Rain vital to the well being of our good earth,
However depressing and wet, always appreciate its true worth.
Rain bouncing on the pavement, running down the street,
The World needs you, you are a most precious and welcome treat.

The Conker Tree

I look out of my hospital window to pass the time away
I spy a large horse chestnut tree, in the summer breeze it does sway.
Its maturity suggests it is 80 or more years old,
It was a thriving strapping long before I was born I am told.
It seeds the conker, has provided our children with many a thrill,
Hitting each other's conker gave them a chance to release their energetic skill.
As evening descends, one sees the occasional loving couple creep under this shady nook,
Declaring their amorous intentions with each other's adoring look.
You see the summer birds fly in and out of this tree,
It provides many a nest, a haven to remain free.
The squirrels keep their young in this wooden giant of yore,
Watching them scuttle about on a branch, the trunk, or foraging on the floor.
Their bushy tails, bright eyes, perky ears, their coats of grey,
Admiring their antics, one could watch them all day.
Night falls, my hospital ward is now going to sleep,
I close my eyes and let dreams into my soul creep,
The world is so full of wonders we rarely do see,
The beauty and life that lives in nearly every tree.

A Glorious Day

It was a day for me of sun, sea and land,
The sun free of cloud shone grand,
The beach was dressed with golden sand,
The ocean waves with their feathered crests displayed their hand.

Today the sea is a little strong, a little frivolous and gay,
With such a fusion of Nature's forces combining, it was going to be a great day.
At high noon, Bob my four-legged pal and I walked around my favourite bay,
For me to relax and enjoy, for Bob to prance in the water and play.

As always the incoming tide means feeding time,
For which the flocks of birds never decline.
A cooling breeze off the sea has arrived,
Along with Bob, here I could happily reside.

We walk along the beach for an hour or more,
Take a rest, my feet are a little sore.
Some pebbles and sharp stone have had their way,
On to their little knives my feet did stray.

The incoming tide has peaked, now the ebb tide
Takes the waters back for an ocean ride.
The sea reflects the blue of the azure sky
The birds having feasted away do fly.

I feel the warm sun, the cool breeze, the jovial tide
Nature today has shown her pleasant side.
I place today with delight in my memory tank,
And wonder if there is anyone up there I should thank.

A Tap on the Window

There was a *tap tap* on the window pane,
It was in the dark of night,
It was too loud to be wind or rain,
I rose from my bed, not without fright.

I nervously pulled back the curtain
Not knowing what I would see,
Nothing friendly or pleasant, that I was certain,
I peered into the darkness wondering what it would be.

Nothing appeared to show the cause of the tap,
We were three floors high, with no window sill,
This uncertainty my determination was beginning to sap,
Was I dreaming, or was I over the hill.

I closed the curtain, went back to bed,
I knew I wasn't going to sleep,
Minutes later the *tap tap tap* on the window came again, it banged through my head,
Its determination drove into my soul most deep.

I grabbed my bible, opened the window wide,
Some one out there needed me, of that I was sure,
I was showing my hand, now they must not hide,
I would try to help, or console, even if I could not cure.

There was stillness such as I could not explain,
I felt a firm hand take mine into theirs,
A quiet voice spoke and was in obvious pain,
"I am so sorry to have caused you so many tears,

Please look into your heart and forgive the sin I have done,
Only with your forgiveness can my soul rest,
In future I will never have a place in the sun,
But my dear Lord will know I have tried my best.

Farewell, dear brother, however you settle the score,
I am in your hands for what my future will be,
You are my kith and kin, whom I still adore,
I pray when we meet again, both hearts will be happy and free.

I lay awake till the dawn did break,
I went to church and prayed in front of the alter,
Forgiving my sister for her most hurtful mistake,
Once given, my promise and fortitude I must not falter.
I am so glad I braved that tap tap tap on the window that night,
It has relieved my mind and put ill will between my sister and me right."

A Penny Please

Please put a penny in the old man's hat,
It won't hurt you, it won't make him fat.
Please put a penny in the old man's hat,
All day on a cold floor he has sat,
Please put a penny in the old man's hat,
Help him to get a comfortable mat.
Please put a penny in the old man's hat,
Don't pass by, not an eyelid bat.
Please put a penny in the old man's hat,
He sleeps on the streets, not a warm flat.
Please put a penny in the old man's hat,
His life is very lonely, would love a chat.
Please put a penny in the old man's hat,
He will smile, thank you, that will be that.
Please put a penny in the old man's hat,
It will help feed him and his old blind cat.
Please put a penny in the old man's hat,
Don't and you could feel like a miserly prat.
Please put a penny in the old man's hat,
Put ten in, go home giving yourself a deserving pat,
Be grateful you don't need a begging hat,
Life certainly is not worth living like that.

Not the Marrying Kind

He is not the marrying kind
Girls catch him if they can
He is not the marrying kind
Girls if they are serious should look for another man.

He is not the marrying kind
He likes the company of ladies and to be in their bed
He is not the marrying kind
Mention marriage and he will run a mile instead.

He is not the marrying kind
You will never get him to the altar
He is not the marrying kind
He is determined not to carry any wedding halter.

He is not the marrying kind
He will tease the girls and have his way
He is not the marrying kind
None of the girls will partner him on their wedding day.

He is not the marrying kind
He won't win a partner who will love him true
Hc is not the marrying kind
When he dies he will be old and very lonely too
He is not the marrying kind
The world won't give a damn, or a too wit to woo.

He had no love to give but only passion to slake
That type of man the world will gladly forsake.
The world needs love in order to survive
To keep us all happy, vibrant and alive.

Hair Cut, Sir?

Billy Joe ran the local barbers called "The Better Snip,"
With his assistant Peter, they both knew how to give a smart clip.
The business had been running now for six years—just over,
They were building up a regular clientele, still not rolling in clover.

In their game barbers with their customers develop a personal relationship
Always cheerful and friendly, careful not to give a painful nip.
One customer Billy Joe got to know quite well
Was Mark, aged thirty-five, who considered himself a swell.

He visited the barbers shop regularly, seemed well-to-do
But impatient to wait if there was a queue.
If the shop was busy he would ask how long he would have to wait,
If twenty minutes he replied, "Sorry, I have another appointment to make."

Billy Joe wondered if he went to Fred's, his competitor down the road,
Because when he left in that direction he always strode.
Several times Mark asked, "How long?" and Billy replied regretfully, "An hour or more."
Mark would smile and say, "Can't wait," and walk out of the door.

Billy Joe was curious, was he losing business to competitor Fred
If not, where did Mark go instead.
Next time Mark called in and saw a queue and said, "How long?"
Billy replied, "At least an hour, I can't be that far wrong."

Mark waved his hand and off he went
Billy Joe had already instructed his assistant to follow this gent.
And see if he goes to Fred for a haircut
Or goes to the golf course for his regular putt.

An hour later Peter reported back and told of his spying
"There is good news and bad as a result of my prying,
The good news is that Mark didn't go to have a haircut with Fred
The bad news is…
When he knew where you were he went to your house and made love to your wife instead."

Cleaned Out

Mary and Joe lived in the little old U.S. of A.
They lived in Maine, retired, and liked to play the lottery.
They rented an old shack and ran an old banger too,
The future was not bright, but what could they do.
Lady Luck smiled on them, they won the lottery, a lot of money,
Decided to buy a new car and move to Florida, the land of milk and honey.
To get there from Maine, they decided to drive in their new car,
After all, ambling along, fifteen hundred miles would not be to far.

Most would have chosen to fly by plane,
With their new car, what a waste, it would be insane.
Good friends and neighbours wished them well and had their say,
Keep on the main roads, and all the road signs strictly obey.
Mary and Joe took this advice and went on their way.
Forty miles on the sign said "CLEAN RESTROOMS AHEAD"
Two months later they arrived in Florida feeling rather dead.
Having cleaned out three hundred and ten restrooms to their total dismay.
Turned round, immediately went back home by plane, determined never
again to come this way.

He Wasn't Meant to Resist!

He looked into her enticing blue eyes,
Her alluring twinkle stirred his thighs.
She was womanhood in a mating state,
He, his manhood desires he urgently needed to sate.
She had met him a few times before,
This was the night she yearned for him inside her bedroom door.
This was the night she wanted him to adore
With his gentleness and heated passion,
Not being able to resist her feminine temptation.
Next morning when the heat of the night had passed away,
It was Mother Nature who had won the day.
The seed had been sown for the next generation
Thus ensuring the growth of the world's population.

Joe Had a Headache

Joe suffered headaches twenty-four hours a day
Whatever pills he took, they wouldn't go away.
In desperation he went to see the appropriate medical authority
An experienced surgeon who could operate with skill and give priority.
He gravely advised the only cure was castration.
Much to Joe's surprise and utter devastation.
"You have a rare disease that puts pressure on your spine,
Generated by germs in your testicles, why, we cannot define."

Joe, desperate, had the necessary operation
It cleared his headaches from pain giving him liberation.
When leaving the hospital, manhood depleted, Joe was depressed
Called in to his tailor for a new suit to be assessed.
The tailor eyed him up and down and said, "Leg 34."
Joe tried it on—a perfect fit to be sure
"How about a new shirt," the tailor said
"A 24 sleeve, a 16 neck," his chest having been read.

Joe spluttered, "You are absolutely right,
With your guidance I will soon be an elegant sight."
The tailor eyed Joe's waist for underwear and uttered, "Size 36"
Joe smiled. "That size is too large and would put me in a fix,
I have worn size 34 for the last five years or more."
The tailor said, "Underwear that tight will make you sore,
It will put great pressure on your spine,
Could possibly cause you severe headaches and make you pine.
You may have to have an operation to soothe your head,
Take my word, be safe, wear 36 instead."

I Am Free

Please don't weep for me, my spirit now flies free,
Please don't weep for me is my earnest plea.
Don't weep for me now I have passed away,
Be strong, make my demise a serene and happy day.

Join me and sing my freedom song,
Celebrating that I am joining heavens joyful throng.
Don't weep for me, I shall soon be walking in the clouds,
Far from the hustle and bustle of the crowds.

Don't weep for me, I shall miss my loved ones and friends most true,
In heaven I will meet old friends and make new.
Don't weep for me I leave behind pain and immobility,
In future I will be torture free and have complete mobility.

Don't weep for me, remember I loved you all,
My departure from earth will enable me to walk free and walk tall.
Don't weep for me, be joyous that I am now free, I'm free, I'm free.

*Written in memory of our son David, who died at the age of seventeen of
Muscular Dystrophy. We cried.*

A Perfect Evening

My rowing boat slips gently into a motionless lake,
Not a ripple or splash does my oar make.
I let the boat drift into deeper waters which remain still,
I rapture to the complete silence, which is tranquil.

The sun in the Western sky is starting to sink,
The evening sky is embossed with blue and pink.
Bourne on calm waters, seductive quiet, beholden to a glorious sunset welcoming night.
I drift, I dream, I relax in nature's composition so enchantingly right.

I rest on my float breathing in the tranquillity,
I deliberate on my life from every possibility.
Night finally closes in, I gently row back to the shore,
I feel rejuvenated, happy, confidence oozes from my every pore.
When Mother Nature is in such a harmonious and benevolent mood as this,
I respond and enjoy her companionship, an opportunity I never miss.

He Died Happy

Mary and Bill had been married forty years,
It had been a satisfactory one, without too many tears.
Once Mary had had her two children early on,
Her desire for passionate love was soon gone.
Bills dream was one day he would meet a woman with fire,
Together they would explode, eager to satisfy each other's desire.
Time passed on and Bill reached retirement age,
His dream was still there, that he could gauge.

At a social evening he met Matilda, a widower, all alone,
Her smiles, her discreet encouragement made his heart beat faster, as men are prone.
They met a few times on the esplanade,
There love grew stronger, did not retard
Then Mary was called away to assist her ailing mother,
A great chance for Bill and Mary to become each other's passionate lover.
That night they went out to dinner and then back to her house,
Once through the front door, no time to play cat and mouse.

Their passion exploded and they went straight to bed,
In the first two hours, three times their climax came to a head,
Their resulting ecstasies came to an end,
When sleep took over and nothing more did they apprehend.
Next morning Bill awoke again feeling a sexual surge,
To continue love making with Matilda he had a renewed urge
Matilda not having had sex for many a year,
Four times in one night, that thought brought her cheer.

After Bill had demonstrated his sexual prowess again,
This time his aging heart could not take the strain.
On this occasion he had a fit, rolled over and died,
The Grim Reaper in the wings was not to be denied.
A few hours later the police officer stood at the dead man's bed,
After Matilda had explained all the circumstances said
"I know it wasn't criminal offence but don't you think your action was a disgrace?"
Without hesitation Matilda replied, "Look at the huge smile on Bill's face, he
thought he was in the best place,
What a way to die, on such a high note,
No pain, no agony, his dream fulfilled, and off to heaven float."

Time to Burn!

To Burnham Beeches I offered to take six of my elderly lady guests,
It would give them a day out, their carers a rest.
Our home has a ten seater bus,
That comfortably takes care of all of us.
At eleven in the morning we were all loaded up to go,
There was a tap on my window which stopped our flow.
An elderly gentleman stood there and said, "Where are you taking
Your ladies today?"
In reply I had this to say,
"I'm taking these ladies to Burnham, what's that to you?"
He quickly replied, "Wait a few moments please and you can burn my
Wife too."

His Choice

An Englishman, a Scotsman and an Irishman work on the top of a London tower block,
The only break they get was lunch time to eat and take stock.
They would sit together, open their lunch boxes, consume and chat,
Talk of every day things like this and that.
One day the Englishman said, "In my sandwiches I have cheese and pickle every day,
For the last fifteen years it has been that way,
I can't stand it anymore, if it continues, tomorrow in this world I will not stay.
I will jump off this tower come what may.

The Scotsman looked into his lunchbox and saw the usual haggis there,
He groaned, bit it, and said it was not fair
Ten years of the same menu, he was not going to stomach any more,
If it was the same too, he too would jump, because he felt so sore.
Murphy the Irishman contemplated his midday snack,
He felt to he was being put on the rack.
When he last had a decent lunch he couldn't hack
If it didn't improve tomorrow he too would jump into the black.

Next day came, no change, so they all jumped off the top,
The tower block being so high they all got their lot.
The next scene is set at their funeral, all buried together.
The three wives sat side by side, discussing why their men's lives they each did sever.
The English man's wife said, "Every Friday I asked George what he would like for
    next week's lunch?
He would always reply, "Same as before, something I could munch."
The Scotsman's wife said, "Jock always wanted his Haggis, that was true,
If I suggested a change his temper just blew."
Murphy's wife listened to the two grieving widows and said in a quiet voice,
"I don't understand Murphy either, he insisted making his own lunch, his choice."

If I Had…

I was wandering down the aisle of the superstore
When I saw a most attractive lass I felt I could adore.
She had long brown hair, blue eyes and a beguiling smile,
She held my total attention all the while.
I wanted to meet her, feel her touch
I wanted to hug her, oh so much.
I left my trolley and followed her to the check out
I waited till she passed through—in my mind there was no doubt.

This was the girl I must get to know
This was the girl who was setting my heart aglow.
I followed her back to her car, took details of her number plate,
I could locate her with this data and in my present state,
I would want to introduce myself and woo
To capture her love in any way I could do.
Next week was Valentine's Day, this would give me a chance
To introduce myself, and my prospects to enhance.

I sent her a bouquet of flowers and a special card too
Saying I wanted to meet her and become her true blue.
I suggested we meet in our local park in the café and have tea,
Hoping we could get on and enjoy each others company.
She rang me, we dated, we met and got on very well,
I come to the end of this story I now tell
Six months later she accepted my proposal of marriage and we are now wed.
Imagine my loss if on that wonderful day I had gone to another superstore instead.

I Want to See the World

I look up into the clear blue sky
I want to be there, flying high.
Free as a bird on the wing
How joyously I would sing, I would sing.

I want to see all of the big wide world
Its beauties, its terrors, its mysteries unfurled.
I want to see a volcano shooting out fire
Watch the grandeur of the Niagara Falls, of that I would never tire.

I want to fly over the Sahara Desert land
And see the camel trains leaving their prints in the sand.
I want to watch the dolphins cavorting in the sea
To see the great herds of buffalo running free.

To see the Himalayan mountains in sparkling white at their best,
To watch mountaineers climbing Everest with all their zest.
To admire the Arctic lights of the Aurora Borealis from the snow below,
Its brilliance will dazzle and set my heart aglow.

To see a tornado with its awesome and dreadful force
Those in front of it, praying it will take another course.
I would want to find out where the rainbow begins
The place in the sky they say to cleanse ones sins.
I want to be a bird and fly and fly and fly,
I want to see all our wonderful world before I die.

God's Face

Mum walked into the lounge and saw her daughter scribbling away,
"High Jane what are you drawing today?"
"I am drawing the face of God," she said,
"I want to finish it before I go to bed."
Mum said, "But no one has ever seen the face of our Dear Lord."
Jane replied, "In that case the face I draw they will all applaud."

Salutation of the Dawn

The salutation of the dawn heralds in a new day,
Yesterday is gone, forever passed away.
Yesterday is a memory, a latent dream,
Our future hopes depend on today and tomorrow it would seem.

Tomorrow brings us hope and expectation,
What we want needs thought and meditation.
When the sun rises and a new day begins,
We pray in that day goodness and love wins.

The glory of the sun brings optimism to us all,
The night brings us rest and time so we might recall.
The salutation of the dawn heralds in a new day,
We pray it will bring joy and contentment our way.

Goodness Gracious Me!

The catholic bishop of Dublin sat enjoying his midday coffee,
Read in his paper Mrs. Murphy had spawned her 14th child and lived in his see.
He called his priest in and said with a big smile,
"This Mrs. Murphy is a catholic according to our file,
Large families born into the catholic faith are always appreciated
They strengthen our faith, and our fellowship increases unabated.
We should acknowledge her efforts in having her 14th boy,
So take this fifty-pound note to this dear lady and increase her joy.

The priest got on his bike and rode twenty miles,
Confident he was going to give Mrs. Murphy a lot of smiles.
Knocked on her door which she opened wide,
Seeing the robed priest she gasped and was open eyed.
He said, " I bring you good news from the Bishop personally,
Your large family will certainly be an asset to the catholic community.,
In appreciation I am instructed to give you this fifty pound note,
Trusting it will bring comfort on the family you dote."

Mrs. Murphy responded, "Three years ago I became a Protestant."
The Priest's mouth dropped open, all energy spent
He spluttered, "Goodness gracious me, you are nothing but a sex maniac, that's
    my view.
On that note I bid you adieu."

The Window Cleaning Man

It was in 1948, four years after the last great war,
Karl arrived at his university in Munich to study law.
He was nineteen, poor, living off a shoestring,
He was prepared to do part time work, to do almost anything.
Cleaning windows he had in mind to sound,
He canvassed a wealthy area to build up a round,
Quickly he found twenty new prospects in this fertile ground.
He was in business, he felt positive he was not going to remain poor,
He mused he was a part-time window cleaner studying law!

The reason he secured this interest so quickly was easy to be found,
Because of the war few men, young or old were not around.
Many had been killed, or returned home injured or maimed,
England and her allies were to be blamed.
Karl worked in the evenings and weekends too,
The war widows, still young, well off, thought this able bodied man would do.
Being deprived of love, getting some now was no sin,
That was what they were interested in.

Hilde, only thirty-two, was attractive and extremely keen
To offer her love, in giving it she was not going to be mean.
Unsuspecting Karl was enticed through her front door,
She quickly seduced him, so passionately, shook him to the core.
That night back in his room he considered his position,
He realised other ladies were in a similar situation.
He had been seduced, his services taken free,
Next time round, anyone needing his services would pay a fee.

Inside a month, he had six ladies lovingly taking him to bed,
They wined and dined him, paid well, better than window cleaning he said.
He gave up cleaning windows, closed the round,
Servicing his ladies took all his spare energies he found.
He developed a charm and grace to woo his nightly amour,
He gave of his best to keep this arrangement secure.
His bank account grew very quickly indeed,
He wasted not, it was to help his future plan to succeed.

For two years he studied hard to get his university degree,
He passed with honours, his certificates were there to see.
Then he went back to his home town well-breeched,
Bidding farewell with charm to all the ladies he had bewitched.
Now back as a solicitor, appearing well off, a new life had begun,
He was welcomed into high society as a new rising sun.
His acquired charm ensured a wealthy woman he did wed,
She was delighted with his attentiveness, kindness, so experienced in bed.

Now in his forties he was asked to give an interview to the press,
Being the richest and most important man in town he was asked to stress,
When in his life time did he start to make his financial progress.
"It was when I took up window cleaning I soon became aware,
Treat all your customers with consideration and care,
So that they will come back for more which is only fair.
It was my window cleaning customers who helped me to succeed,
Because I gave them the quality service that they were in need
Take care and give your customers all you have got,
That's the only way to succeed whether you like it or not!

…Ing

Have you ever thought about the word-ending ING?
It always seems to be involved with something
Firemen use it constantly, ringing the bells *ding-a-ling, ding-a-ling*
Children need it when they are playing
Choruses utilise it when they are singing
Cargo ships are involved with the goods they are bringing
Architects need it when they measure with a piece of string
Anglers are grateful for it when they go fishing

Judges capitalise on it when they are sentencing
Agriculturalists need it to carry on their farming
Betting men risk their money with their gambling
Church goers exercise their voices with their praising
Soccer fans watch their skilful players footballing
Scotsmen sword-dance whilst having a Highland fling
City men make fortunes with their banking
Soldiers keep fit with intensive training

Dustmen keep our towns dirt-free with road cleansing
Bakers produce our daily bread with their baking
Winter sportsmen on mountain slopes enjoy skiing
Authors, poets and musicians writing, writing, writing
Carers look after us with their dedicated nursing
Drunks and layabouts when in ill-mood cursing
Diplomats in difficult situations placating
Politicians as always promising, promising, promising
Comedians doing their best to keep their audiences laughing
So on and on goes this word ending in ING
It seems without it we can hardly do anything!

A Wink Will Do!

Did you see the builder down the road?
Working in the hot sun, virtually unclothed.
I must admit his handsome torso caught my attention.
Stirring my heart and other parts not to mention.
It's twelve o'clock, I must pass the site again,
Doing so I don't really know what I will gain.
Maybe I must be getting broody,
I am certainly not miserable or moody.
Still I shall put on my short skirt and busty bra,
Swagger slowly past the building site, hoping to raise a little hoo-ha,
If he gives me a wink, I will return a smile,
If he chat's me up, I will give him a fair trial.
If he does not see me first time, I will walk past again,
If he does not see me then, I will know my efforts have been in vain.

A Breath of Spring Air

A breath of spring air
Makes young maidens' expectation of life raise,
A breath of spring air
Makes ardent young lovers sing the ladies' praise.
A breath of spring air
Makes the ladies preen themselves, take extra care,
A breath of spring air
Makes young men strut and display their manly ware.
A breath of spring air
Makes our lasses put on their most beguiling smile
A breath of spring air
Makes the young men perk up their loving style.
A breath of spring air
Makes the ladies view their competitors with distain
A breath of spring air
Makes young men their passion to contain
A breath of spring air
Makes the gentle sex desire to have a family
A breath of spring air
Makes the male desire to prove his paternity
A breath of spring air
Makes the ladies ensure they will with children procreate
A breath of spring air
Makes young men desire to settle down and mate
In our village there are eight young ladies who wish to enter the marriage state
Only seven suitors are available to keep that date,
One of our angels will be full of despair,
When she realises there is not another left to love her and care.

Six Wild Stallions

Six stallions galloping, galloping wild and free
They were galloping, galloping to frolic in the sea.
They came from the hills not far away
Now they were thundering in our quiet sandy bay.

They were vibrant, energetic, handsome and strong,
They bathed in the sea, they seemed to belong.
They galloped along the shoreline's golden sand,
Six wild stallions in their prime, looking simply grand.

At the end of the bay they sauntered and came to a stop,
Resting, deciding when to take the return gallop.
The leader stamped his hoof; it was time to go,
They galloped and galloped in a seemingly effortless flow.

They galloped and galloped these six stallions wild and free,
They had enjoyed their visit down to the sea.
They galloped back to their home in their valley and hill,
Their visit to our beach always gives us a thrill.

Walking on Air

My new found love and I walk down the Strand,
He gently and firmly takes hold of my hand,
I am walking on air, I feel so grand.
We only met last week, it was not planned.
It was in the library, we were both looking for a book,
I was perusing my subject, I sensed his look.
He came over to ask for advice,
I smiled, and answered, he seemed very nice.

He chattered me up to my delight,
He suggested we went walking next Sunday, I said, "Alright!"
It took ages for the week to pass,
I kept looking in the diary and the looking glass,
Planning what to wear, to be as casual as one can be,
Trying to dress in some form of harmony.
We met at the gates down by the Strand,
All young ladies like me will understand
When a young man you fancy is taking you out,
You give him your fullest attention without doubt.

We walked down the Strand, he gently and firmly took my hand,
I was walking on air, I simply felt grand.

I Want to Be Loved

I want to be loved, my love to only love me,
My true love would make me as happy can be.
I want to be loved, to be worry free,
My true love will adore and marry me.

Together we would love and be trouble free,
The future would be ours, as far as we could see.
I want him to hug me, show me he is a man,
I will love him as much as any woman can.

I want to be loved, no longer alone in the dark,
My future would be joyous, never stark.
I want to be loved and caressed at every turn,
His loving to be gentle and cherishing, never stern

I want to be loved by my one and only true love,
I would walk on air and fly in the clouds above.
I want to be loved, is it too much
Dear lord, for you to grant me love as such?

o o o

Thank you for reading my poems. I hope that you enjoyed them and that they brought pleasure to you.

I enjoyed writing them.

Thank you.

Terry Godwin

o o o

Printed in the United Kingdom
by Lightning Source UK Ltd.
107578UKS00002BA/1-51